10
Performance-Based
Projects

Grades 3–5

10 Performance-Based Projects for the Math Classroom

Todd Stanley

PRUFROCK PRESS INC.

WACO, TEXAS

Prufrock Press Inc.
P.O. Box 8813
Waco, TX 76714-8813
Phone: (800) 998-2208
Fax: (800) 240-0333
http://www.prufrock.com

TABLE OF CONTENTS

INTRODUCTION

Why Project-Based Learning?

Twenty-first century skills, or survival skills, as termed by Tony Wagner in his book *The Global Achievement Gap* (2014), involve students being able to do more than memorize facts and instead apply skills and, more importantly, problem solve (Stoof, Martens, Van Merriënboer, & Bastiaens, 2002). In short, teachers are tasked with the difficult job of trying to create thinkers. This results from businesses complaining that the best and brightest students that the educational system is sending their way are very intelligent but woefully inept at figuring out problems, arguing students know a lot of "facts" but are not "competent" (Bastiaens & Martens, 2000). Any teacher able to help students become these thinkers would be providing them with an advantage when they enter the real world.

The educational system has to do a better job of preparing students to solve real-world problems. How do we do that in the current system of standards and testing? With so much at stake on these achievement tests, the bigger question is: How often in life are we asked to take a pencil-and-paper test? Not very often unless you count online personality quizzes. In real life we are usually dealing with projects, either at work, home, or other settings. If we truly want to get students ready for the real world, we should be teaching them how to handle the real-world dilemma of a project.

As mentioned in *Project-Based Learning for Gifted Students: A Handbook for the 21st-Century Classroom* (Stanley, 2012), according to the Buck

Institute for Education, research studies have demonstrated project-based learning can:

* increase academic achievement on standardized assessment tests;
* teach math, economics, social studies, science, medical skills, and health-related subjects more effectively than traditional teaching methods;
* increase long-term retention of knowledge, skill development, and student and teacher satisfaction;
* prepare students to integrate and explain concepts better than traditional instructional methods;
* prove especially helpful for low-achieving students;
* present a workable model for larger school reform; and
* help students to master 21st-century skills such as communication, independent and critical thinking, and research. (p. 4)

This is why project-based learning is such a good fit for creating such thinkers. It has been discovered that students:

* prefer to structure their own tasks they are working on and establish deadlines as opposed to having the teacher assign them (Dunn & Dunn, 1984; Renzulli & Smith, 1982; Stewart, 1980);
* learn more and retain content more accurately when allowed to work on projects in which they set the pace (Whitener, 1989);
* show an increased benefit in learning when they teach each other through projects (Kingsley, 1986; Johnsen-Harrris, 1983);
* show improvement in cooperative learning skills when working in groups because they must work together to solve problems (Peterson, 1997); and
* show increased engagement after participating in PBL than students who did not (Grant & Branch, 2005; Horton et al., 2006; Johnston, 2004; Jones & Kalinowski, 2007; Ljung & Blackwell, 1996; McMiller, Lee, Saroop, Green, & Johnson, 2006; Toolin, 2004).

Based on this research, a better question to ask is not why use project-based learning, but rather why not use project-based learning?

What Are the Advantages of Using PBL in a Mathematics Classroom?

Project-based learning is an excellent vehicle to teach 21st-century skills. In *21st-Century Skills: Learning for Life in Our Times* (2009), Bernie Trilling and Charles Fadel mentioned, among valuable 21st-century skills, eight specific skills that PBL can effectively teach:

1. public speaking,
2. problem solving,
3. collaboration,
4. critical thinking,
5. information literacy,
6. creativity,
7. adaptability, and
8. self-direction. (p. viii)

Math lends itself to problem solving, the very nature of math. Combining this with project-based learning, problem solving becomes relevant. For example, if you teach students that *2 + 2 = 4*, it is an abstract form, merely a group of numbers that combine to make a different number. But the problem can be more concrete: *Bobby has two pieces of gum and Greg has two pieces of gum. How much gum do they have if they combine them?* Now the 4 becomes more than a number; it becomes potentially more gum, something you can literally sink your teeth into. If you apply mathematical problem solving to a real-world problem, then students will benefit because they see how it can be used. In an episode of *The Simpsons* titled "The Dead Putting Society" (Martin, 1990), Lisa tries to help Bart become better at miniature golf, so that he can win a bet for his father:

Lisa: The basis of this game is simple geometry. Just hit the ball here.
(Bart does so and gets a hole in one.)
Bart: I can't believe it. You've actually found a practical use for geometry.

Getting students to think about mathematics in the real world and solving real-world problems will enable students to better understand math. Just like Bart, they may find a practical use for it. This ties in to many Common Core State Standards for Mathematics (CCSS-M) for grades 3–5, such as:

1. 3.OA.D.8 Solve two-step word problems using the four operations. Represent these problems using equations with a letter standing for the unknown quantity. Assess the reasonableness of answers using mental computation and estimation strategies including rounding.

2. 3.MD.D.8 Solve real world and mathematical problems involving perimeters of polygons, including finding the perimeter given the side lengths, finding an unknown side length, and exhibiting rectangles with the same perimeter and different areas or with the same area and different perimeters.

3. 5.NF.A.2 Solve word problems involving addition and subtraction of fractions referring to the same whole, including cases of unlike denominators, e.g., by using visual fraction models or equations to represent the problem. Use benchmark fractions and number sense of fractions to estimate mentally and assess the reasonableness of answers.

4. 5.NF.B.6 Solve real world problems involving multiplication of fractions and mixed numbers, e.g., by using visual fraction models or equations to represent the problem.

5. 4.OA.A.3 Solve multistep word problems posed with whole numbers and having whole-number answers using the four operations, including problems in which remainders must be interpreted. Represent these problems using equations with a letter standing for the unknown quantity. Assess the reasonableness of answers using mental computation and estimation strategies including rounding.

Critical thinking is also key. This is problem solving at a higher level of thinking. Most educators are familiar with Bloom's taxonomy. The lower level thinking skills are represented by:

1. remembering,
2. comprehending, and
3. applying.

There is a lot of *applying* in math, applying mathematical concepts and formulas and solving a problem using them. But how much higher level thinking are we doing in math? Many students find math difficult to understand. However, this does not mean it is at a higher level of thinking. You can give a student the following problem: *2.769 times 10 to the negative third power equals what?* This problem may cause one to pause in solving it (the answer is .002769, by the way), but students are still using the principle of application, a lower level thinking skill. Thinking at a higher level means accessing the following thought processes:

- analyzing,
- evaluating, and
- creating.

Consider this problem: *A number of children are standing in a circle. They are evenly spaced and the seventh child is directly opposite the 18th child. How many children are there altogether?* You would have to really *analyze* the situation and break it down. You would first have to figure out that because the seventh and 18th child are directly opposite one another, that represents half of the circle and half of the children. You can figure this out by subtracting 7 from 18 to get 11. In order to get the entire circle, we would need to double it ($11 \times 2 = 22$.) The answer is that 22 students make up the circle. There is some knowledge used here (knowing that the two are directly across from each other means they make up half of the circle), some application (being able to figure out how to arrive at the number of half by subtracting one from the other), but in order to answer the question, you have to analyze the situation and break it apart in order to solve it.

That is the tricky part of math—making questions that challenge students to analyze, evaluate, and create. They are not as easy to write as lower level questions, but they ensure that students truly understand the mathematical concepts because they can use them in any situation. One way to do this is to use verbs of higher level questioning. For example, these verbs are usually indicative of lower level questions:

1. **Remembering:** count, define, describe, draw, find, identify, label, list, match, name, quote, recall, recite, record, select, sequence, tell, view, write
2. **Comprehending:** cite, conclude, demonstrate, describe, discuss, estimate, explain, generalize, illustrate, paraphrase, predict, report, restate, review, summarize, tell

3. **Applying:** apply, change, chart, choose, classify, compute, construct, prepare, produce, relate, report, select, show, solve, transfer, use

Higher level questioning usually includes the following verbs:
1. **Analyzing:** analyze, break down, characterize, classify, compare, contrast, debate, deduce, diagram, differentiate, discriminate, distinguish, examine, illustrate, outline, prioritize, relate, research, separate, subdivide
2. **Evaluating:** appraise, argue, assess, choose, conclude, critique, decide, defend, evaluate, interpret, judge, justify, predict, prioritize, prove, rank, rate, select, support
3. **Creating:** categorize, compose, construct, create, design, develop, formulate, generate, integrate, invent, make, modify, organize, perform, plan, produce, propose, reorganize, rewrite

You have to be careful because just using the verb does not make the question a higher level one. For example, you can say: *Assess what 2 + 2 equals.* This is still a lower level question. You have to make sure the content of the question matches the verb that you use. Because you are using real-world problems in your project-based learning, getting students to think at a higher level will be much easier to achieve. Notice the verbs in these CCSS-M for grades 3–5:
1. 3.MD.B.4 Generate measurement data by measuring lengths using rulers marked with halves and fourths of an inch. Show the data by making a line plot, where the horizontal scale is marked off in appropriate units—whole numbers, halves, or quarters.
2. 3.NF.A.3d Compare two fractions with the same numerator or the same denominator by reasoning about their size. Recognize that comparisons are valid only when the two fractions refer to the same whole. Record the results of comparisons with the symbols >, =, or <, and justify the conclusions, e.g., by using a visual fraction model.
3. 4.MD.B.4 Make a line plot to display a data set of measurements in fractions of a unit ($\frac{1}{2}, \frac{1}{4}, \frac{1}{8}$). Solve problems involving addition and subtraction of fractions by using information presented in line plots. For example, from a line plot find and interpret the differ-

ence in length between the longest and shortest specimens in an insect collection.

4. 4.G.A.2 Classify two-dimensional figures based on the presence or absence of parallel or perpendicular lines, or the presence or absence of angles of a specified size. Recognize right triangles as a category, and identify right triangles.

5. 5.MD.C.5 Relate volume to the operations of multiplication and addition and solve real world and mathematical problems involving volume.

An ancillary 21st-century skill that project-based learning provides in math is collaboration. Because math typically involves the teacher assigning problems that a student must then solve, it usually involves working by oneself. Yes, it is true; math is the loneliest subject because often you are working alone. By turning your mathematics classroom into a project-based learning environment, there will be more opportunities for students to work in groups. Collaboration is a valuable 21st-century skill that:

1. develops higher level thinking skills;
2. provides students with greater ability to view situations from others' perspectives;
3. addresses learning style differences among students;
4. resembles real-life social and employment situations in the classroom;
5. creates an environment of active and involved inquiry learning;
6. develops social interaction skills;
7. encourages student responsibility for learning;
8. stimulates critical thinking;
9. helps students clarify ideas through discussion and debate;
10. enhances self-management skills;
11. establishes an atmosphere of cooperation and helping;
12. allows for modeling of problem-solving techniques by students' peers;
13. creates environments where students can practice building leadership skills;
14. builds self-esteem in students; and
15. develops students' oral communication skills.

Using project-based learning in your mathematics classroom will enable you to provide students with these benefits.

What Sorts of Products Could Be Used in a Mathematics Classroom?

As laid out in *Performance-Based Assessment for 21st-Century Skills* (Stanley, 2014), there are 10 different types of assessments that can be used in a project-based learning environment:

1. oral presentations,
2. debates/speeches,
3. role playing,
4. group discussions,
5. interviews,
6. portfolios,
7. exhibitions,
8. essays,
9. research papers, and
10. journals/student logs. (p. 43)

There are, of course, many other types, but these are the 10 this book will be focusing on and providing examples of.

Keep in mind these project plans can be changed, added to, rearranged, and anything else you need to do to make them effective for your students. There are some that contain lessons that could be used for other projects, so move aspects around and set them up the way that works best for your students.

1 Oral Presentation

Much of what a student knows can be expressed in an oral presentation. Classrooms are full of the type of student who raises his hand and can provide insightful, meaningful responses when taking part in discussion, but as soon as you ask that same student to write down his thoughts, you are lucky to get a one- or two-word written response. He is not able, or more likely, not willing, to give you the same insightful responses in writing. In dealing with these kinds of students, the question for me became: Why couldn't this student provide his answers orally, especially if it meant getting responses like he did in class? On the flip side are those students who do not know how to express themselves in an oral presentation, and the acquisition of the skill is very valuable to them.

What It Looks Like

Oral presentations can take several forms, but they typically consist of an informative speech designed to educate an audience. Some of the forms can be:

- an individual or group report,
- an oral briefing,
- an oral exam,
- a panel discussion, or
- an oral critique.

The student's goal in an oral presentation is to verbally teach classmates or the audience what she has learned after researching a particular topic or skill. A successful oral presentation needs to be set up just like an essay would, with a topic sentence, supporting details, and several drafts before the final presentation. This structure is something that should be taught to students. This can be done with modeling, looking at exemplary examples of great oral presentations, or practicing presentations with no consequences.

Having Your Math and Eating It Too

Baking a cake or cookies involves math, especially fractions. How much of each ingredient to put in, what measurement for those ingredients, how long to bake, how much will it make, and so on, are all factors.

In this project, students will work in groups to bake a product, using various kinds of math. Each group will bring its product and recipe to share with the class. Their recipes must involve math problems that others must solve in order to determine the amount of ingredients to use. They will teach the class using the problems they create, demonstrating equivalent fractions, adding and subtracting fractions with different denominators, and multiplying and dividing fractions.

Connections to CCSS

- 4.NF.A.1
- 4.NF.A.2
- 4.NF.B.3
- 4.NF.B.4

Materials

- Project Outline: Having Your Math and Eating It Too (student copies)
- Suggested Timeline
- Lesson: Using a Recipe
- Lesson: The Basics of Fractions

- Lesson: Adding and Subracting Fractions With Different Denominators
- Lesson: Multiplying Fractions by Whole Numbers
- Lesson: What Makes a Good Presentation?
- Handout 1.1: Chocolate Chip Cookie Recipe (student copies)
- Handout 1.2: Fractions (student copies)
- Handout 1.3: Different Denominators (student copies)
- Handout 1.4: Multiplying Fractions by Whole Numbers (student copies)
- Handout 1.5: What Makes a Good Presentation? (student copies)
- Handout 1.6: Peer Review (student copies)
- Product Rubric (student copies)

PROJECT OUTLINE

Having Your Math and Eating It Too

Directions: Baking a cake or cookies involves math, especially fractions. How much of each ingredient to put in, what measurement for those ingredients, how long to bake, how much will it make, and so on, are all factors.

You and your group will bake a product, using various kinds of math. You will bring your product to share with the class. Your recipe must involve math problems that others must solve in order to determine the amount of ingredients to use. You will teach the class using the problems you create, demonstrating equivalent fractions, adding and subtracting fractions with different denominators, and multiplying and dividing fractions. In other words, if the recipe calls for three eggs, that would be three out of 12 (a dozen), or $\frac{1}{4}$ of a carton of eggs. You will also alter your recipe to feed more or less people, doubling the recipe and splitting it in half.

You have a few choices when it comes to presenting your recipe. The most important of these is that you demonstrate the math involved in the project, providing examples for all three of the learning objectives. Here are some suggestions for what you could do:

- Bring in the finished product for sampling and prepare the recipe using actual ingredients up until the cooking aspect.
- Bring in the finished product for sampling and mock prepare the recipe.
- Present your recipe and what you would do if preparing it, showing the math involving fractions.

SUGGESTED TIMELINE

DAY				
1 Introduce the project (bring in a baked good to share) with Lesson: Using a Recipe (see Handout 1.1).	**2** Conduct Lesson: The Basics of Fractions, and distribute Handout 1.2.	**3** Conduct Lesson: Adding and Subtracting Fractions With Different Denominators, and distribute Handout 1.3.	**4** Conduct Lesson: Multiplying Fractions and Whole Numbers, and distribute Handout 1.4.	**5** Have students form groups and identify a recipe involving at least five fractions.
6 Have groups analyze their recipe's fractions.	**7** Have groups analyze their recipe's fractions.	**8** Have groups complete analyzing their recipe's fractions.	**9** Have groups double their recipe and/or split it in half.	**10** Have groups double their recipe and/or split it in half.
11 Conduct Lesson: What Makes a Good Presentation, and distribute Handout 1.5.	**12** Groups need to prepare their presentations.	**13** Groups need to prepare their presentations.	**14** Groups need to prepare their presentations.	**15** Groups need to practice their presentations and conduct peer reviews with another group (see Handout 1.6).
16 Begin group presentations (see Product Rubric).	**17** Continue group presentations.	**18** Continue group presentations.		

LESSON

Using a Recipe

Bake chocolate chip cookies for your class, using the recipe below. As the students are enjoying their cookies, distribute Handout 1.1: Chocolate Chip Cookie Recipe.

Ingredients

- $2\frac{1}{4}$ cups all-purpose flour
- 1 teaspoon baking soda
- 1 teaspoon salt
- 1 teaspoon vanilla extract
- 1 cup (2 sticks) butter, softened

- $\frac{3}{4}$ cup granulated sugar
- $\frac{3}{4}$ cup packed brown sugar
- 2 large eggs
- $2\frac{3}{4}$ cups of chocolate chips

Directions

1. Preheat oven to 375°F.
2. Combine the baking soda and salt in a small bowl.
3. Mix in the butter, sugar, brown sugar, and vanilla.
4. After this is mixed to a creamy texture, add each egg and mix them in as well.
5. Add flour gradually, mixing as you add.
6. Stir in the chocolate chips.
7. Use a spoon to create little batter balls, and spread them out on a baking sheet.
8. Bake for 9 to 11 minutes.
9. Cool on the sheet for a few minutes before removing them to wire racks.
10. Once cooled (or even if a little warm), enjoy.

Tell students to note all of the fractions in the recipe. Use this to demonstrate the three learning objectives they need to demonstrate in their projects:

- **Equivalent fractions:** The $\frac{1}{2}$ cup of chocolate chips remains the same whether you divide the cup into halves or fourths. In other words, $\frac{1}{2}$ cup would be equivalent to two $\frac{1}{4}$ cups.

- **Comparing fractions with different denominators:** Compare two fractions with different numerators and different denominators by creating common denominators or numerators, or by comparing to a benchmark fraction such as $\frac{1}{2}$. Recognize that comparisons are valid only when the two fractions refer to the same whole. Record the results of comparisons with symbols and/or justify the conclusions by using a visual fraction model. For example, 3 teaspoons is 1 tablespoon.

- **Multiplying fractions by a whole number:** To double the recipe, everything needs to be multipled by 2:

  ◇ $2\frac{1}{4}$ cups all-purpose flour = $4\frac{1}{2}$ cups

  ◇ 1 teaspoon baking soda = 2 teaspoons

  ◇ 1 teaspoon salt = 2 teaspoons

  ◇ 1 teaspoon vanilla extract = 2 teaspoons

  ◇ 1 cup (2 sticks) butter, softened = 2 cups (4 sticks)

  ◇ $\frac{3}{4}$ cup granulated sugar = $1\frac{1}{2}$ cups

  ◇ $\frac{3}{4}$ cup packed brown sugar = $1\frac{1}{2}$ cups

  ◇ 2 large eggs = 4 large eggs

  ◇ $2\frac{3}{4}$ cups of chocolate chips = $5\frac{1}{2}$ cups

- **Dividing fractions by a whole number:** To halve the recipe, everything needs to be divided by 2:

  ◇ $2\dfrac{1}{4}$ cups all-purpose flour = $1\dfrac{1}{8}$ cups

  ◇ 1 teaspoon baking soda = $\dfrac{1}{2}$ teaspoon

  ◇ 1 teaspoon salt = $\dfrac{1}{2}$ teaspoon

  ◇ 1 teaspoon vanilla extract = $\dfrac{1}{2}$ teaspoon

  ◇ 1 cup (2 sticks) butter, softened = $\dfrac{1}{2}$ cup (1 stick)

  ◇ $\dfrac{3}{4}$ cup granulated sugar = $\dfrac{3}{8}$ cup

  ◇ $\dfrac{3}{4}$ cup packed brown sugar = $\dfrac{3}{8}$ cup

  ◇ 2 large eggs = 1 large egg

  ◇ $2\dfrac{3}{4}$ cups of chocolate chips = $1\dfrac{3}{8}$ cups

The Basics of Fractions

Tell students that one way to think of fractions is that they are pieces of a whole.

For example, if you have $\frac{3}{4}$, the whole is broken into four parts, using the bottom number, the denominator. The numerator is the number of sections of the whole that the fraction takes up. That means three of the four sections represent the numerator:

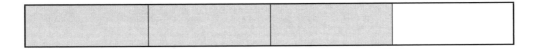

The denominator always represents the whole no matter what number is used. So if there is a fraction of $\frac{9}{12}$, the denominator is still represented by the whole, it is simply divided up into 12 parts instead of the 4 from the previous answer:

Even though these two fractions have different numbers, they take up the same amount of space in the whole. This is known as being equivalent to one another.

Distribute Handout 1.2: Fractions, allowing students time to complete the problems. After going over the answers, ask: *What did you notice about answers 1 and 7, as well as 6 and 8?* Tell students that even though they were different numbers, the fractions still equaled the same on the bar graph. This means they are equivalent to one another. In their recipes, students will have to have some fractions that use different numbers but are equivalent to one another.

Adding and Subtracting Fractions With Different Denominators

Ask students: *How do you add and subtract fractions that have different numerators and denominators? In other words, how can you possibly add these two fractions?*

$$\frac{1}{2} + \frac{3}{4}$$

It is not as simple as just adding the numbers. In order to add or do any sort of math with fractions, you have to create the same denominator. That means finding a number that both numbers can divide into. In this case both 2 and 4 divide into 4, so 4 will be the denominator:

$$\frac{2}{4} + \frac{3}{4}$$

The numerator of the changed denominator also has to be altered to match however much you increased it. So by changing the 2 to a 4, you doubled the number, thus you have to double the top numerator as well.

$$\frac{2}{4} + \frac{3}{4} = \frac{5}{4}$$

Distribute Handout 1.3: Different Denominators, allowing students time to complete the problems.

Multiplying Fractions by Whole Numbers

In order to multiply a fraction by a whole number you need to convert the whole number to a fraction. This allows you to multiply. It is very simple to convert a whole number to a fraction. The number becomes the numerator, and the denominator is simply 1.

$$\frac{2}{3} \times 4 = \frac{2}{3} \times \frac{4}{1}$$

You then multiply the numerator by the other numerator and the denominator with the other denominator:

$$2 \times 4 = 8$$
$$3 \times 1 = 3$$

$$\frac{2}{3} \times 4 = \frac{8}{3}$$

Distribute Handout 1.4: Multiplying Fractions by Whole Numbers, allowing students time to complete the problems.

What Makes a Good Presentation?

There are certain elements that make up a good oral presentation. Distribute Handout 1.5: What Makes a Good Presentation? and review the 10 things for students to consider:

1. Keep consistent eye contact.
2. Use a strong, confident voice.
3. Avoid "umms," "ahhhs," and "likes."
4. Keep your hands in the correct place. (Don't put them in your pockets or cross your arms.)
5. Don't read your information. Present it.
6. Show you care about your topic. (Don't use a monotone voice.)
7. Stand up straight.
8. Be prepared. (Practice ahead of time.)
9. Maintain professionalism. (Don't giggle or say inappropriate things.)
10. Have a flow to your presentation. (Have notes to fall back on if you get stuck.)

Have students watch an example of a good cooking presentation. Good examples that can be found on YouTube include:

- Nerdy Nummies
- Emeril Lagasse
- Julia Child
- Martha Stewart
- Iron Chef
- Gordon Ramsey

Have students watch and go through the list on Handout 1.5, identifying whether or not the presenter met all of the requirements of a good presentation.

Presentation Days

Set up a schedule for when students will present, giving them an allotted time. Tell students which day they are presenting on so they can make arrangements to bring in their supplies and materials. When all groups have presented, collect the recipes students used and create a class recipe book, which can be given to students and parents.

HANDOUT 1.1

Chocolate Chip Cookie Recipe

Directions: Analyze this chocolate chip cookie recipe. What do you notice about the fractions in the ingredients list? How would you make the recipe for more people? Fewer people?

Ingredients

- $2\frac{1}{4}$ cups all-purpose flour
- 1 teaspoon baking soda
- 1 teaspoon salt
- 1 teaspoon vanilla extract
- 1 cup (2 sticks) butter, softened

- $\frac{3}{4}$ cup granulated sugar
- $\frac{3}{4}$ cup packed brown sugar
- 2 large eggs
- $2\frac{3}{4}$ cups of chocolate chips

Directions

1. Preheat oven to 375°F.
2. Combine the baking soda and salt in a small bowl.
3. Mix in the butter, sugar, brown sugar, and vanilla.
4. After this is mixed to a creamy texture, add each egg and mix them in as well.
5. Add flour gradually, mixing as you add.
6. Stir in the chocolate chips.
7. Use a spoon to create little batter balls, and spread them out on a baking sheet.
8. Bake for 9 to 11 minutes.
9. Cool on the sheet for a few minutes before removing them to wire racks.
10. Once cooled (or even if a little warm), enjoy.

HANDOUT 1.2

Fractions

Directions: Represent each fraction on a bar graph.

1. $\frac{1}{2}$

2. $\frac{5}{16}$

3. $\frac{9}{10}$

4. $\frac{2}{5}$

5. $\frac{4}{6}$

6. $\frac{3}{5}$

7. $\frac{7}{14}$

8. $\frac{6}{10}$

HANDOUT 1.3

Different Denominators

Directions: Add the fractions.

1. $\dfrac{1}{2}+\dfrac{3}{6}$

2. $\dfrac{2}{3}+\dfrac{3}{4}$

3. $\dfrac{4}{5}+\dfrac{1}{3}$

4. $\dfrac{1}{4}+\dfrac{5}{6}$

5. $\dfrac{2}{5}+\dfrac{2}{4}$

6. $\dfrac{4}{4}+\dfrac{2}{3}$

7. $\dfrac{2}{6}+\dfrac{1}{2}$

8. $\dfrac{3}{4}+\dfrac{3}{5}$

9. $\dfrac{1}{5}+\dfrac{3}{3}$

10. $\dfrac{6}{10}+\dfrac{6}{4}$

HANDOUT 1.4

Multiplying Fractions by Whole Numbers

Directions: Use multiplication to solve the following problems.

1. $\frac{1}{2} \times 2$

2. $\frac{3}{5} \times 4$

3. $\frac{2}{3} \times 5$

4. $\frac{3}{4} \times 3$

5. $\frac{2}{4} \times 6$

6. $\frac{1}{3} \times 7$

7. $\frac{4}{5} \times 3$

8. $\frac{1}{2} \times 4$

9. $\frac{2}{3} \times 3$

10. $\frac{3}{4} \times 8$

Name: _____ Date: _____

HANDOUT 1.5

What Makes a Good Presentation?

Directions: There are certain elements that make up a good oral presentation. Here are 10 things to consider.

1. Keep consistent eye contact.

2. Use a strong, confident voice.

3. Avoid "umms," "ahhhs," and "likes."

4. Keep your hands in the correct place. (Don't put them in your pockets or cross your arms.)

5. Don't read your information. Present it.

6. Show you care about your topic. (Don't use a monotone voice.)

7. Stand up straight.

8. Be prepared. (Practice ahead of time.)

9. Maintain professionalism. (Don't giggle or say inappropriate things.)

10. Have a flow to your presentation. (Have notes to fall back on if you get stuck.)

Name: _____ Date: _____

HANDOUT 1.6

Peer Review

Directions: Circle whether or not the other group's members were successful at the following.

Group Members' Names: _____

Group's Recipe: _____

1.	They kept consistent eye contact.	Yes	No
2.	They used a strong, confident voice.	Yes	No
3.	They did not use "umms," "ahhhs," and "likes."	Yes	No
4.	They used their hands correctly (not in their pockets or arms crossed).	Yes	No
5.	They presented their information; they did not read it.	Yes	No
6.	They care about their topic (no monotone voice).	Yes	No
7.	They stood up straight.	Yes	No
8.	They were prepared (practiced ahead of time).	Yes	No
9.	They maintained professionalism (no giggling or saying inappropriate things).	Yes	No
10.	Their presentation flowed (and they had notes to fall back on if they get stuck).	Yes	No

PRODUCT RUBRIC

Having Your Cake and Eating It Too

Overall	Mathematics	Presentation
Excellent (A)	◆ Group correctly demonstrates two or more examples of a part of the recipe using equivalent fractions. ◆ Group correctly demonstrates two or more examples of a part of the recipe where they compare fractions with different denominators/numerators. ◆ Group correctly demonstrates how to halve the recipe and to double it.	◆ Group presents itself in a professional manner, showing maturity throughout the presentation. ◆ Group consistently speaks with confidence in their presentation. ◆ Each group member contributes to the presentation, explaining some portion of the recipe and the fractions involved.
Good (B–C)	◆ Group correctly demonstrates an example of a part of the recipe using equivalent fractions. ◆ Group correctly demonstrates an example of a part of the recipe where they compare fractions with different denominators/numerators. ◆ Group correctly demonstrates how to halve the recipe or to double it.	◆ Group most of the time presents itself in a professional manner, but does not maintain this through the entire presentation. ◆ Group speaks with confidence in their presentation most of the time, but are not consistent throughout. ◆ Most group members contribute to the presentation, explaining some portion of the recipe and the fractions involved, but not all.
Needs Improvement (D–F)	◆ Group does not correctly demonstrate a part of the recipe using equivalent fractions. ◆ Group does not correctly demonstrate a part of the recipe where they compare fractions with different denominators/numerators. ◆ Group neither correctly demonstrates how to halve the recipe nor to double it.	◆ Group does not present itself in a professional manner, showing lack of maturity throughout the presentation. ◆ Group does not speak with confidence in their presentation, looking unsure of themselves. ◆ One or two group members dominate the presentation, explaining most of the recipe and the fractions involved while others are not involved.

② Debate/ Speech

This is another form of oral presentation, but instead of seeking to inform, the main goal is to persuade. Debates and speeches are a higher level of thinking because they don't just convey information but employ tactics to convince someone that one student's opinions or viewpoints are more valuable than another's. It is a process more complicated than the usual presentation because it looks at "ethos, the credibility of the speaker; logos, the logical proof and reasoning presented in the words of the speech; and pathos, the use of emotional appeals to influence the audience" (Brydon & Scott, 2000).

What It Looks Like

Debates are especially great to use when the concept being taught is ambiguous or allows for multiple perspectives. Speeches are another form of this persuasive oral presentation. While delivering a speech, the student is either playing a role or representing a organization. He must convince people of his platform or ideals. Although not as interactive as a debate, the speech still requires the student to tap into higher levels of thinking and make a sound argument.

Design Your Own Waterpark

Who doesn't like the waterpark? With slides, tunnels, whirlpools, and whatever else, there is something for everyone.

In this project, students will work in groups to create their own waterpark that provides entertainment for as many different people as possible. They must develop rides and attractions, as well as determine the depth of each pool and calculate the volume and how much water will be needed. They should create a floor plan for this waterpark or even a model of what it will look like. Each group will present its waterpark to "investors," an authentic audience of your choosing, convincing them to build its waterpark.

Connections to CCSS

- 5.MD.C.4
- 5.MD.C.5
- 5.MD.C.5.c

Materials

- Project Outline: Design Your Own Waterpark (student copies)
- Suggested Timeline
- Lesson: What Is Volume?
- Lesson: How Much Water Is in the Bathtub?
- Lesson: What Makes a Good Waterpark?
- Lesson: Giving a Professional Presentation
- Handout 2.1: Volume (student copies)
- Handout 2.2: Tips for Giving a Professional Presentation (student copies)
- Product Rubric (student copies)

Name: _____ Date: _____

PROJECT OUTLINE

Design Your Own Waterpark

Directions: Who doesn't like the waterpark? With slides, tunnels, whirlpools, and whatever else, there is something for everyone. How much water do you suppose it takes to fill up all of the pools at the local swimming pool or a larger park like Great Wolf Lodge?

You and your group must create your own waterpark that provides as much entertainment for as many different people as possible. That means you will have a kid section, a teen section, an adult section, and maybe even a senior citizen section in your park. These different parts will be of different depths, depending on the group of people or activities going on in each. In addition to creating the rides and attractions, you must determine the depth of each pool and calculate the volume of how much water will be needed. You should create a floor plan for this waterpark or even a model of what it will look like. Your group will present this waterpark to investors, convincing them to build your waterpark.

SUGGESTED TIMELINE

DAY				
1 Introduce the project and conduct Lesson: What Is Volume?	**2** Have students complete Handout 2.1: Volume.	**3** Conduct Lesson: How Much Water Is in the Bathtub?	**4** Conduct Lesson: What Makes a Good Waterpark?	**5** Have students form groups and begin brainstorming.
6 Have students continue brainstorming.	**7** Have groups begin a rough draft of their waterparks.	**8** Have groups complete a rough draft of their waterparks.	**9** Instructor or group checks the math involved in the rough draft.	**10** Have groups begin final drafts of their plans or building models.
11 Have groups continue final drafts of their plans or building models.	**12** Have groups continue final drafts of their plans or building models.	**13** Have groups continue final drafts of their plans or building models.	**14** Have groups continue final drafts of their plans or building models.	**15** Conduct Lesson: Giving a Professional Presentation (see Handout 2.2).
16 Have groups develop speeches for investors.	**17** Have groups develop speeches for investors.	**18** Have groups practice speeches.	**19** Have groups practice speeches.	**20** Have groups present speeches to an authentic audience (see Product Rubric).

What Is Volume?

Tell students that volume is the amount of space that is taken up within three-dimensional objects. It uses the following formula: $L \times W \times H$. In its simplest form, they can use this formula to determine the volume of a cube.

Demonstrate solving for volume, with a cube that is 3 in. tall, 4 in. long, and 2 in. wide. In this case, you would multiply the length of 4 by the width of 2, giving you 8. You would then take this total of 8 and times it by the height which is 3 for a total of 24.

Tell students: *One way to think of this is to imagine the above three-dimensional shape is made up of lots of little cubes which represent its volume. Each cube is 1 x 1 x 1 and you are trying to determine how many of these cubes would make up the three-dimensional object.*

The length would look like this:

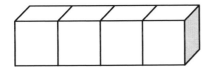

The width would look like this:

And the height would look like this:

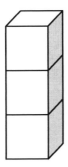

When you fill the entire three-dimensional object with these cubes, it would look like this:

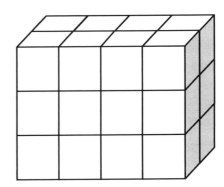

This gives the object 24 cubes, matching the volume we got when we used the formula of $L \times W \times H$.

LESSON

How Much Water Is in the Bathtub?

Finding volume on a worksheet is one thing, but being able to find it in the real world is another. Tell students: *You are presented with a volume problem every single day (hopefully) whenever you take a bath. The problem is, how much water fits into your bathtub? How do you determine this? We are going to look at a bathtub and determine the volume of it.*

Display a doll bathtub or other kind of model of a bathtub for students to use.

In groups, have students develop a plan to gather the data needed to determine how much water is needed to fill the tub. Students will need something to measure with so that they can determine the width, height, and depth of the bathtub being used. From this students should be able to determine the volume of the tub with the three correct measurements.

Have students report their answers and how they arrived at the answer they got.

To take it a step further, have them determine how long it would take for the bathtub to fill up based on this volume.

What Makes a Good Waterpark?

Remind students that their groups will need to decide how many pools they will have at their waterpark and what size they will be. Although not as important, they will also need to decide what will make a waterpark that people will want to come to. They are trying to convince people to invest in their waterparks, so having attractions that would bring people in would be a must.

As students begin planning their parks, share the following tips for designing their floor plans:

- Use graph paper if possible (can also design on the computer).
- Use proper drawing tools (i.e., ruler, compass, etc.).
- Use a pencil for the initial drawing and then go over with pen.
- Color your model design.
- Include dimensions for the model.
- Label the different parts of the design, writing clearly in print.
- Make the design large enough for others to tell what it is.

Giving a Professional Presentation

Share with students a couple of presentations that students can watch to act as an exemplar for their own. Examples of good presentations include:

- Steve Jobs's presentations, such as: https://www.youtube.com/watch?v=X5yRhO SL_-c
- Gordon Kangas's TED Talk, "Giving Presentations Worth Listening To," https://www.youtube.com/watch?v=NUXkThfQx6A
- Michelle Obama's speeches, such as https://www.youtube.com/watch?v=6CbDe aqBA7c

The presentation should be appropriate for the age of the class and also should be engaging.

Distribute Handout 2.2: Tips for Giving a Professional Presentation and review it with students.

HANDOUT 2.1

Volume

Directions: Find the volume of the following figures.

1.

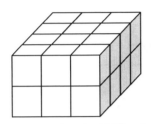

4.

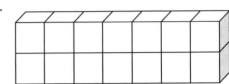

2.

5.

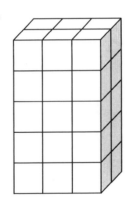

3.

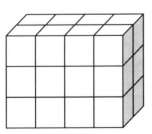

6.

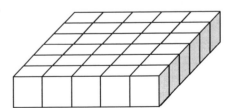

HANDOUT 2.2

Tips for Giving a Professional Presentation

Directions: Consider the following tips as you prepare your presentation.

1. **Prepare:** Do your homework and prepare your speech ahead of time.

2. **Organize:** Structure your speech into a few main parts.

3. **Practice:** Practice, practice, practice.

4. **Look the part:** If you look professional, people will think you are professional.

5. **Present:** Don't just read your presentation. It should be as though you are having a conversation.

6. **Go slow:** Even slower than that.

7. **Use aids:** Only if they are adding something to your presentation.

8. **Act the part:** If you act professional, people will think you are professional.

9. **Involve the crowd:** Make eye contact with the audience.

10. **Finish strong:** Have a satisfying conclusion that leaves the audience thinking.

Note. Adapted from *15 Strategies for Giving Oral Presentations* by L. F. Jacobs & J. S. Hyman, 2010, retrieved from http://www.usnews.com/education/blogs/professors-guide/2010/02/24/15-strategies-for-giving-oral-presentations.

Name: _____ Date: _____

PRODUCT RUBRIC

Design Your Own Waterpark

Overall	Design	Mathematics	Speech
Excellent (A)	◆ Design looks professional; group used a straight edge and color to bring it to life. ◆ One can clearly tell where everything is going to be located, as there are labels and captions. ◆ One of the pools is displayed using unit cubes to show its volume in a three-dimensional drawing/model.	◆ Design has at least four pools for which the volume is correctly determined. ◆ Three different units of measurement are used to determine the volume of the pools. ◆ Group correctly determines how many gallons of water it will take to fill all of the pools in the waterpark.	◆ Group presents itself in a professional manner, showing maturity throughout the speech. ◆ Group consistently speaks with confidence. ◆ Group uses many effective methods to persuade those listening to choose their waterpark design.
Good (B–C)	◆ Design looks professional; group used a straight edge and color to bring it to life, but there are a couple of sloppy aspects. ◆ One can tell where most everything is going to be located, as there are labels and captions, but there are a couple instances where they are needed. ◆ One of the pools is displayed using unit cubes to show its volume in a two-dimensional drawing/model.	◆ Design has at least four pools for which the volume is determined and most, but not all, are correct. ◆ Two different units of measurement are used to determine the volume of the pools. ◆ Group makes an attempt to determine how many gallons of water it will take to fill all of the pools but is off a little with the math.	◆ Group presents itself in a professional manner most of the time, but does not maintain this through the entire speech. ◆ Group speaks with confidence most of the time, but is not consistent throughout. ◆ Group uses many methods to persuade those listening to choose their waterpark design but not all are effective or convincing.

Product Rubric: Design Your Own Waterpark, *continued*

Overall	Design	Mathematics	Speech
Needs Work (D–F)	• Design of waterpark looks sloppy; group did not use a straight edge and/or color to bring it to life. • It is difficult to tell where everything is going to be located because there are few to no labels and captions. • None of the pools are displayed using unit cubes to show its volume.	• Design has less than four pools for which the volume is determined, or most of them are not correct. • Only one unit of measurement is used to determine the volume of the pools. • Group does not make an attempt to determine how many gallons of water it will take to fill all of the pools in the waterpark or is not even close in the math.	• Group does not present itself in a professional manner, showing lack of maturity throughout the speech. • Group does not speak with confidence in their speech, looking unsure of themselves. • Group only uses one method or does not really try to persuade those listening to choose their waterpark (does not really make an argument for it).

3 Group Discussion

Discussions can take what is being learned to a higher level. There are two types of group discussions. One involves students participating and answering with very surface-level responses. The discussion dies on the vine before it can bloom. It looks like a discussion, but it certainly does not feel like one. There is usually no energy, no passion, and, although you might get the information you seek from students, no depth. The second type of group discussion is one in which students cannot wait to participate because what they want to share is burning a hole in their minds. It may require some content knowledge, but it also requires tapping into experiences and opinions. This is the type of discussion you want to have in your classroom.

What It Looks Like

An easy way to make a group discussion meaningful is to make sure the questions being asked are higher level questions. If you are looking for discussions to generate close-ended, knowledge-based information, it becomes a hunt-and-peck event, where you are simply looking for someone to provide the correct answer. If, however, the questions are open-ended, higher level questions designed to be cracked open and explored, the discussion will be meaningful. Some of this involves preparing challenging, higher level questions ahead of time. This also means being able to generate these higher level questions in response to what a student has said. It requires a teacher to be able to think quickly on her feet and ask appropriate follow-up questions to mine all of the meaningful lessons from a conversation.

Group discussions do not need to be led by the teacher. Teachers often feel the need to be the ones steering the ship so that it will head in the direction they want it to go, but sometimes the most interesting trips involve detours. In this case, allowing the discussion to wander to seemingly unrelated topics or to allow students to explore ideas you had not even considered might actually produce better results than you expect. Dividing the students into groups and providing them with a few guiding questions to get the discussion going can lead to these results. Without the teacher there, students might provide more creative answers instead of searching for the answer they believe the teacher is looking for.

Grading a discussion can be a little challenging, but taking copious notes on how a student responds and his level of understanding, or even recording the discussion for you to go back to later are methods you can use to assess a discussion.

Going on a Trip, Pioneer Style

In this project, students will work individually or in groups to road-trip to the Western United States in the year 1850. They will plot out what roads/trails they will take to reach their final destination in the West, how many miles they will travel, where they will stay along the way, and other details. Because there are no stores along the way, they also must figure out how much food and water to bring in order to survive. They will need to submit a budget for how much water and food they are going to bring. Then, they will present their itinerary and supply list to a group of students and lead a discussion about how successful they believe the trip will be.

Connections to CCSS

- 3.MD.A.1
- 3.MD.A.2

Materials

- Project Outline: Going on a Trip, Pioneer Style (student copies)
- Suggested Timeline
- Lesson: Introduction to Westward Expansion
- Lesson: How to Estimate and Measure Time and Distance
- Lesson: How to Estimate and Measure Volume of Liquids
- Lesson: Food and Other Trip Supplies
- Lesson: How to Lead a Good Discussion
- Handout 3.1: How Long the Trip Is Going to Take (student copies)
- Handout 3.2: How Much Liquid to Bring (student copies)
- Handout 3.3: How Much Supplies Weigh (student copies)
- Handout 3.4: Preparing for Your Discussion (student copies)
- Handout 3.5: Peer Review (student copies)
- Handout 3.6: Student Reflection (student copies)
- Group Discussion Assessment Form (teacher's copies)
- One-on-One Discussion Assessment Form (teacher's copies)

PROJECT OUTLINE

Going on a Trip, Pioneer Style

Directions: Road trips can seem spontaneous, but they are often well-planned, with reservations made at hotels and scheduled stops here and there. Even pioneers in the olden days had to plan out their trips carefully for fear they would not survive.

You will plan a road trip to the Western United States in the year 1850. You will plot out what roads/trails you will take to reach your final destination in the West, how many miles will you travel, where you will stay along the way, and other details. Because there are no stores along the way, you also must figure out how much food and water to bring in order to survive. You will need to submit a budget for how much water and food you are going to bring. Then, you will present your itinerary and supply list to a group of students and lead a discussion about how successful they believe your trip will be.

SUGGESTED TIMELINE

DAY				
1 Introduce project and conduct Lesson: Introduction to Westward Expansion.	**2** Have students play "Westward Trail" online.	**3** Have a class discussion about the experiences on "Westward Trail."	**4** Have students (or groups) select destinations.	**5** Conduct Lesson: How to Estimate and Measure Time and Distance (see Handout 3.1).
6 Have teams research the distance they must travel and complete Handout 3.1.	**7** Have teams research the distance they must travel and complete Handout 3.1.	**8** Have teams research the distance they must travel and complete Handout 3.1.	**9** Conduct Lesson: How to Estimate and Measure Volume of Liquids (see Handout 3.2).	**10** Have teams research how much water they need to bring and complete Handout 3.2.
11 Conduct Lesson: Food and Other Trip Supplies (see Handout 3.3).	**12** Have teams estimate how many supplies they are going to need for the trip and complete Handout 3.3.	**13** Have teams estimate how many supplies they are going to need for the trip and complete Handout 3.3.	**14** Have teams estimate how many supplies they are going to need for the trip and complete Handout 3.3.	**15** Conduct Lesson: How to Lead a Good Discussion (see Handout 3.4).
16 Have teams work on their presentations and complete Handout 3.4.	**17** Have teams work on their presentations and complete Handout 3.4.	**18** Have teams work on their presentations and complete Handout 3.4.	**19** Begin student discussions (see Handout 3.5: Peer Review, Group Discussion Assessment Form).	**20** Conduct student discussions.

DAY				
21 Begin student reflection discussions (see Handout 3.6: Student Reflection, One-on-One Discussion Assessment Form).	**22** Conduct student reflection discussions.			

Introduction to Westward Expansion

Traveling across the United States can be a daunting task. From dealing with traffic to finding a cheap place to stay, it can be quite a challenge. Tell students to imagine it is 150 years ago and they have to travel across the United States. There are no cars, hotels, or even any bridges. How far will they have to travel overland to get to their destination? How long will this take? How many supplies will they have to take?

Tell students: *You will be traveling around 1850, which means you will either be using the Santa Fe Trail, Oregon Trail, or the California Trail to get where you are going. You must plan a trip for at least five people overland to your destination. You will have to determine many things for your trip, which you will present to the class.*

1. How many miles will you be traveling?

2. How long will it take you to travel this distance?

3. How much food will you need to bring?

4. How much water will you need to bring?

5. How many other supplies will you need?

6. How much is all of this going to weigh?

7. How much will you be able to carry?

Westward Trail Simulation

Have students play the online simulation game *Westward Trail* to get an idea of what they are going to be doing: http://www.globalgamenetwork.com/westward_trail.html.

After students have played the simulation, you should conduct a class discussion about their successes and failures:

1. Did you feel you had enough supplies to make the trip? If not, what would you have changed in the supplies you brought?

2. What sort of supplies do you think would have been valuable? What would have been better left behind?

3. What obstacles did you encounter and how did you overcome them?

4. Why would it be important to pick the right time to go on the trail?

5. How is the prospect of running into a river different then than it is now?

6. Did everyone in your party survive the trip? Do you think this was realistic?

7. Would you have made a trip such as this in 1850, now knowing the dangers and problems you might encounter?

8. Why would a trip like this seem so dangerous? Is it as dangerous nowadays? Why or why not?

9. Are there things we take for granted now that they didn't have back then? (i.e. cars, bridges, rest stops, hotels, etc.)

10. Why was travel such as this so important?

Selecting Destinations

Have students randomly select one of these from slips of paper, or assign them at random. This list includes the starting point and the destination:

- St. Louis, MO, to Salt Lake City, UT
- Chicago, IL, to Denver, CO
- Council Bluffs, IA, to Phoenix, AZ
- Scottsbluff, NE, to Oregon City, OR
- New York, NY, to Whitman, MO
- Independence, MO, to Los Angeles, CA
- San Antonio, TX, to San Diego, CA
- Columbus, OH, to Santa Fe, NM
- Kansas City, MO, to Portland, OR
- Independence, MO, to Sutter's Fort, CA

How to Estimate and Measure Time and Distance

Tell students they need to figure out how many miles it is from their starting point to their destination. For example, famous explorers Lewis and Clark started in St. Louis, MO, and ended on the Pacific Coast, where modern-day Washington is located.

Using a map of Lewis and Clark's expedition, tell students they are not going to be able to find an exact distance between the two points but can get a general idea. Ask: *How can we do that with the tools this map has provided us with?*

Using the map's scale, students can determine approximately how many miles Lewis and Clark's trip took. Demonstrate how to use the scale to determine the distance, using the edge of a piece of paper or other straight edge. You can estimate that the trip was about 2,000 miles.

Tell students: *For much of their trip, Lewis and Clark had a boat and used the waterways for faster travel. You will be traveling by horse and wagon, which is a bit slower. So, if we were taking the Lewis and Clark route by wagon, we need to estimate how much time it would take. Here is the formula you will use:* On average a wagon can travel 12 miles in a day. *How would you figure out how much time it is going to take?*

You divide the number of miles the trip is going to take by the amount of miles you can cover in a day:

$$2000 \div 12 = 167 \text{ days to complete the trip}$$

Did it take Lewis and Clark that much time? It actually took them 1 year, 6 months, and 1 day. How many total days would that be?

$$365 + 180 + 1 = 546 \text{ days}$$

Tell students that Lewis and Clark had to stop often for the snow to melt in the mountain passes so they could travel, and there were no established trails when they made their journey, meaning they spent a lot of time cutting their way through forests. Although students are determining an estimate of the amount of time it will take, they are assuming that nothing will go wrong, affecting their 12 miles a day.

Lesson: How to Estimate and Measure Time and Distance, *continued*

Tell students: *The problem you are trying to solve is: If it is ____ miles to your destination, and you travel 12 miles a day, how many days will it take you to arrive at your destination? In addition, you will need to know how long it takes to travel a single mile.* Ask students:

1. How many hours are in a day? (24 hours.)

2. Will you be traveling that entire time? (No.)

3. What will most likely determine when you travel? (When it is light out.)

4. How many hours of daylight are there in a day? (Anywhere from 10 hours to 14 hours depending on the time of the year.)

5. How far could you travel each hour if you had 9 hours of daylight? ($9 \div 12 = 0.75$ of a mile an hour.)

Tell students there are some things they should consider when they prepare their presentations:

1. Are there physical obstacles you might encounter that will make your trip go slower?

2. Are there waterways you can take that might make your trip go faster?

3. What about the weather? Could that make for slower traveling?

4. What is your party makeup? Do you have any women who could possibly get pregnant?

5. What are some other things that might cause delays in the trip?

Distribute Handout 3.1: How Long the Trip Is Going to Take for students to complete.

How to Estimate and Measure Volume of Liquids

When measuring liquid volumes there are different units of measurement used than if measuring other masses. Tell students: *Liquid is measured in volume. If you think of soda, there are 12-ounce cans, 24-ounce bottles, or 2-liter bottles. Large bottles of water are measured in gallons. The large tank in a water cooler is 5 gallons of water.*

Liquids need to be placed in a container in order to transport, so really you are measuring how much liquid can fit into the container. Here are examples of ways to measure liquids:

- **Barrels:** Barrels can be dry barrels or fluid barrels, such as oil and water barrels. The specific amount of volume a barrel holds has differed over time and depending on the type. In the U.S., a beer barrel is around 31 gallons, while an oil barrel is around 42 gallons.
- **Gallons:** A gallon is equal to 128 ounces, 4 quarts, 8 pints, or about 3.785 liters.

For your overland trip, you will be dealing with larger quantities of liquid, so most of your supplies will be measured in gallons.

Food and Other Trip Supplies

Distribute Handout 3.3: How Much Supplies Weigh and tell students: *Let us take a look at some of the camp supplies Lewis and Clark brought on their trip and how much it all weighed. The chart on Handout 3.3 is from Clark's actual journal.*

After students have completed Handout 3.3, discuss their responses, as well as some of the other supplies Lewis and Clark took on their expedition. They took many things, such as:

- **Mathematical Instruments:** surveyor's compass, hand compass, quadrants, a telescope, thermometers, two sextants, a set of plotting instruments, and a chronometer (needed to calculate longitude).

- **Camp Supplies:** 150 yards of cloth to be oiled and sewn into tents and sheets, pliers, chisels, 30 steels for striking to make fire, handsaws, hatchets, whetstones, iron corn mill, 24 tablespoons, mosquito curtains, $10\frac{1}{2}$ pounds of fishing hooks and fishing lines, 12 pounds of soap, 193 pounds of "portable soup" (a thick paste concocted by boiling down beef, eggs, and vegetables), three bushels of salt, writing paper, ink, and crayons.

- **Presents for Indians:** 12 dozen pocket mirrors, 4,600 sewing needles, 144 small scissors, 10 pounds of sewing thread, silk ribbons, ivory combs, handkerchiefs, yards of bright-colored cloth, 130 rolls of tobacco, tomahawks that doubled as pipes, 288 knives, 8 brass kettles, vermilion face paint, and 33 pounds of tiny beads of assorted colors.

- **Clothing:** 45 flannel shirts, coats, frocks, shoes, woolen pants, blankets, knapsacks, and stockings.

- **Arms and Ammunition:** 15 prototype Model 1803 muzzle-loading .54 caliber rifles, knives, 500 rifle flints, 420 pounds of sheet lead for bullets, 176 pounds of gunpowder packed in 52 lead canisters, and 1 long-barreled rifle.

- **Medicine and Medical Supplies:** 50 dozen Dr. Rush's patented "Rush's pills", lancets, forceps, syringes, tourniquets, 1,300 doses of physic, 1,100 hundred doses of emetic, 3,500 doses of diaphoretic (sweat inducer), and other drugs for blistering, salivation, and increased kidney output.

Tell students: *They carried many of these items for the 8,000 miles round trip and the 3 years it took them. You need to consider what other items you will need to take that are essential to the success of your trip. You also have to anticipate any problems you might encounter and what supplies will help you overcome these problems.*

How to Lead a Good Discussion

Share with students the following tips for good discussions:

- Ask a question that causes people to think because it does not have an obvious answer.
- Be prepared, have questions written out beforehand.
- Don't judge the responses (provide a safe environment).
- Don't let one person dominate the discussion; try to involve all participants.
- Listen as much if not more than you speak.
- Be willing to ask follow-up questions to further the conversation.
- Be enthusiastic about your topic.
- Summarize important points.

Distribute Handout 3.4: Preparing for Your Discussion for students to complete.

Discussion Days

Tell students that in order to share and discuss their trips, they will be broken into groups at stations around the room (e.g., five stations, each with someone leading the discussion and an audience). They will be given an allotted amount of time to conduct their discussion and then rotate the audience and speakers until everyone has had multiple chances to lead and take part in a discussion.

After each round of discussion is over, audience members will fill out evaluations for how they felt the discussion went on Handout 3.5: Peer Review. As the teacher, you may want to move about the room and record your observations during discussions.

Project 3: Group Discussion

HANDOUT 3.1

How Long the Trip Is Going to Take

Directions: Find a map of your trip or find the two points of travel on a map. Draw or paste that map below, and complete the following questions.

1. Using the scale, estimate how many miles the trip is going to take.

2. If you travel an average of 12 miles per day, how many days will the trip take?

3. Figure out how many miles per hour you would need to travel in a 10-hour day in order to reach 12 miles a day.
   ◇ 11-hour day:

   ◇ 12-hour day:

   ◇ 13-hour day:

   ◇ 14-hour day:

HANDOUT 3.2

How Much Liquid to Bring

Directions: Members of your travel party will need plenty of water to complete the journey. Answer the following questions.

1. How many people are in your party?

2. Each member of your party needs to drink half a gallon a day. How many gallons will you need per day for your party?

3. How many days is your trip going to take?

4. How many gallons of water will you need over the course of the entire trip?

5. If there are 42 gallons in a barrel of water, how many barrels will you need to bring on the trip?

Name: _____   Date: _____

HANDOUT 3.3

How Much Supplies Weigh

Directions: Take a look at some of the food and other supplies Lewis and Clark brought on their trip and how much it all weighed. The following chart is from Clark's actual journal. Answer the following questions about your observations.

14 bags of parchmeal	1200	1 bag of coffee	50
9 bags of common parchmeal	800	1 bag of beans & 1 of peas	100
11 bags of corn, hulled	1000	2 bags of sugar	112
1 bag of candlewick	8	1 keg of hogs lard	100
24 bushels of Natchies Corn huled	1344	4 barrels of corn hulled	600
7 barrels of salt pork	750	1 barrel of meal	150
50 kegs of pork	3705	600 lb. of grees	600
30 half barrels of flour, 3 bags of flour	3900	7 bags of biscuits, 4 barrels of biscuits	650
2 boxes of candles 70 lb. and about 50 lb. (one of which has 50 lb. of soap)	170	50 bushels of meal	2500

1. How many pounds is this in total?

2. If there are 0.453592 kilograms in a pound, how many kilograms did Lewis and Clark take?

3. How many grams?

4. There were 33 people on the Lewis and Clark expedition. If you divided all of these supplies equally how many kilograms would each person carry?

Handout 3.3: How Much Supplies Weigh, *continued*

5. William Clark said in his journals "It requires 4 deer, or an elk and a deer, or one buffalo to supply us for 24 hours". Each man consumed 9 pounds of meat a day. How many pounds of animals did they have to kill a day?

6. One man died on the trip from what is believed to have been appendicitis. Once he died, how many pounds a day of meat did they need to get?

How Much Food to Bring on Your Journey

Directions: Answer the following questions, considering the supplies you will bring on your journey.

1. How many people are in your party?

2. If each member of your party eats 9 pounds of meat a day, how much meat will you need per day for your party?

3. How many days is your trip going to take?

4. How many pounds of meat will you need over the course of the entire trip?

5. If there are 74 pounds of pork in a keg, how many kegs will you need to bring on the trip?

Name: _____ Date: _____

HANDOUT 3.4

Preparing for Your Discussion

Directions: Use the following prompts to prepare for your discussion. You should know the answers to the first 10 questions and be ready to think about and discuss the next 10 questions.

Estimations for Your Trip

1. How many miles is your trip?

2. How did you arrive at this estimation?

3. How long do you estimate the trip will take you?

4. How did you arrive at this estimation?

5. What volume of liquids are you estimating to take on your trip?

6. How did you arrive at this estimation?

Handout 3.4: Preparing for Your Discussion, *continued*

7. How many pounds of food are you estimating to take on your trip?

8. How did you arrive at this estimation?

9. What are some other essential items you will need to bring with you?

10. Why are these items so important to the success of your trip?

Discussion Questions to Consider

1. Do you think this party will have enough food and/or water?

2. What do you think the chances for survival are?

3. What could be done to improve the chances of this trip being a success?

4. Would you want to make the trip they have planned?

5. Do you think the estimates made for food and water are realistic?

6. Is there something this group is overlooking that will be important for their trip?

7. What problems do you see this group running across in their travels?

8. Have they taken everything into account?

9. Will they be prepared if something goes wrong?

10. How would you plan this trip differently if you had to do it again?

Name: _____ Date: _____

HANDOUT 3.5

Peer Review

Directions: Check the box you feel best describes how the student's discussion went.

Peer's Name: _____ Peer's Story: _____

- ☐ The student asked mostly basic questions that resulted in short, one-sentence answers.
- ☐ The student asked some basic questions that resulted in short answers but from time to time asked a question that sparked some deeper discussion.
- ☐ The student consistently asked questions that caused me to think about the point of view, leading to further discussion but did not ask follow-up questions to expand it.
- ☐ The student consistently asked questions that caused me to think about the point of view, leading to further discussion and follow-up questions that expanded it.

Peer's Name: _____ Peer's Story: _____

- ☐ The student asked mostly basic questions that resulted in short, one-sentence answers.
- ☐ The student asked some basic questions that resulted in short answers but from time to time asked a question that sparked some deeper discussion.
- ☐ The student consistently asked questions that caused me to think about the point of view, leading to further discussion but did not ask follow-up questions to expand it.
- ☐ The student consistently asked questions that caused me to think about the point of view, leading to further discussion and follow-up questions that expanded it.

Peer's Name: _____ Peer's Story: _____

- ☐ The student asked mostly basic questions that resulted in short, one-sentence answers.
- ☐ The student asked some basic questions that resulted in short answers but from time to time asked a question that sparked some deeper discussion.
- ☐ The student consistently asked questions that caused me to think about the point of view, leading to further discussion but did not ask follow-up questions to expand it.
- ☐ The student consistently asked questions that caused me to think about the point of view, leading to further discussion and follow-up questions that expanded it.

HANDOUT 3.6

Student Reflection

Directions: Answer the following reflection questions with lots of detail to support your opinions.

1. What would you give yourself as a grade for this project? Justify your evaluation.

2. What did you like about the project?

3. What did you dislike about the project?

Handout 3.6: Student Reflection, *continued*

4. If you could change anything about the project, what would it be and why?

5. If you had to redo this project, would you do anything differently? Why?

6. What is one thing you feel you did really well during this project?

7. What did you learn from others during this project?

Group Discussion

Directions: Put an X or mark where the student is on the scale.

Comprehension	Application	Analysis/Synthesis	Evaluation
Student has basic understanding, but when asked to go deeper, he or she struggles to make connections.	Student has a basic understanding and can apply what he or she has learned to a situation but does not bring anything new or insightful to the discussion.	Student has a deeper understanding than just the basics and can build on others' ideas but does not justify decisions with evidence.	Student understands at a deeper level and justifies decisions with sound evidence.

Student's Name: _____

←———————|———————|———————|———————→

Student's Name: _____

←———————|———————|———————|———————→

Student's Name: _____

←———————|———————|———————|———————→

Student's Name: _____

←———————|———————|———————|———————→

Student's Name: _____

←———————|———————|———————|———————→

ASSESSMENT FORM

One-On-One Discussion

Directions: Put an X or mark where the student is on the scale.

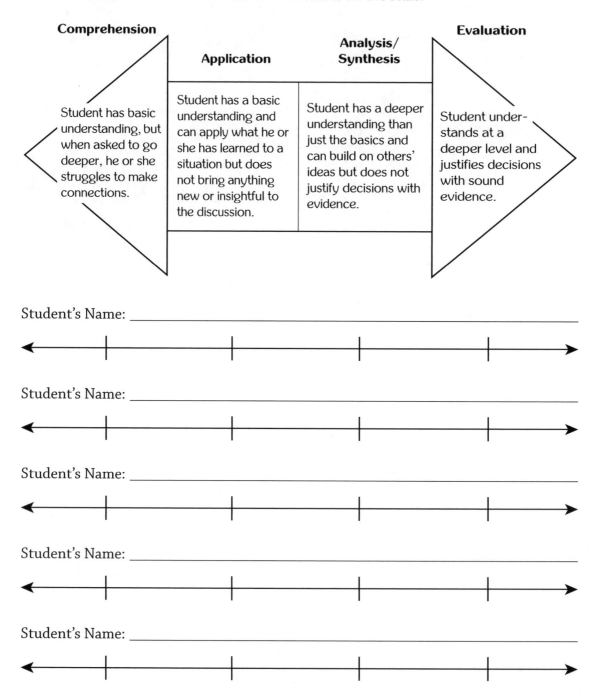

Comprehension

Student has basic understanding, but when asked to go deeper, he or she struggles to make connections.

Application

Student has a basic understanding and can apply what he or she has learned to a situation but does not bring anything new or insightful to the discussion.

Analysis/ Synthesis

Student has a deeper understanding than just the basics and can build on others' ideas but does not justify decisions with evidence.

Evaluation

Student under- stands at a deeper level and justifies decisions with sound evidence.

Student's Name: _____

⟵ —|——————|——————|——————|— ⟶

Student's Name: _____

⟵ —|——————|——————|——————|— ⟶

Student's Name: _____

⟵ —|——————|——————|——————|— ⟶

Student's Name: _____

⟵ —|——————|——————|——————|— ⟶

Student's Name: _____

⟵ —|——————|——————|——————|— ⟶

4 Role-Playing

Role-playing is a form of creative oral presentation where a student must inhabit a specific persona and carry out the role from that person's perspective. It allows students to walk a day in the shoes of someone else and helps them to understand different perspectives. A constant struggle with students is to get them to think about anything from another perspective than their own. Giving them opportunities to explore other perspectives will allow them to gain a better understanding of a character, time period, or idea.

What It Looks Like

Role-playing can involve having a person assume the role of a character from a novel to demonstrate how he would react to situations the character had to experience. Or it can involve a mock trial in which a student is given a specific role to play, such as a lawyer, a witness, a defendant, the judge, or even the jury. Although a student is focusing in on her specific role, she is getting an understanding of how a trial works and of the arguments being made.

Playing Store

In this project, students will work in groups to simulate opening a store that sells specific items (i.e., clothing, toys, tools, etc.). They will sell these items, offering sales (i.e., 30% off or half off). They will work at the store, while classmates are the customers, exchanging money back and forth.

Connections to CCSS

- 5.NBT.B.7

Materials

- Project Outline: Playing Store (student copies)
- Suggested Timeline
- Lesson: Going to the Store
- Lesson: Working With Decimals
- Lesson: Calculating Sales Tax and Discounts
- Handout 4.1: Decimals (student copies)
- Handout 4.2: Sales Tax and Discounts (student copies)
- Handout 4.3: Inventory Sheet (student copies)
- Handout 4.4: Invoice Sheet (student copies)
- Handout 4.5: Student Reflection (student copies)
- Product Rubric (student copies)

Supplemental Materials

- Materials to demonstrate a store (items to sell, marbles/chips/board game money to act as currency)

PROJECT OUTLINE

Playing Store

Directions: When you go to the store to buy groceries or clothing, everything you purchase is added up, discounts and taxes are factored in, and a total is given. Today, this is all done by scanners and computers, but just a couple of decades ago, this had to be figured out by people.

You and your group will open a store that sells specific items (i.e., clothing, toys, tools, etc.). You will sell these items, offering sales (i.e., 30% off or half off). You will work at the store, while other classmates are the customers, exchanging money back and forth. Set up the store, open for business, and see how much money you make. You will keep a running tally that you will turn in at the end, along with your reflections of what went well, what did not, and what you learned.

Members of your group will take on the following roles:

- **Cashier:** Responsible for ringing up the cost of items and giving proper change.
- **Tax:** Responsible for tabulating the tax on the total purchase.
- **Manager:** Responsible for balancing the cash register money to the receipts.
- **Sales:** Responsible for figuring out the price of sale items.

SUGGESTED TIMELINE

DAY				
1 Introduce the project and conduct Lesson: Going to the Store.	**2** Conduct Lesson: Working With Decimals, and distribute Handout 4.1.	**3** Complete and review Handout 4.1.	**4** Conduct Lesson: Calculating Sales Tax and Discounts, and distribute Handout 4.2.	**5** Complete and review Handout 4.2.
6 Have students break into groups and begin planning the type of store they wish to open.	**7** Have groups begin selecting their inventory (see Handout 4.3).	**8** Have groups continue selecting their inventory.	**9** Have groups determine their inventory (if they will bring in real items or create them).	**10** Have groups determine their inventory (if they will bring in real items or create them).
11 Have groups determine their prices and discounts.	**12** Have groups set up their store and practice running it (see Handout 4.4).	**13** Have groups set up their store and practice running it (see Handout 4.4).	**14** Have groups open for business, running their store and visiting others' (see Handout 4.4, Product Rubric).	**15** Have groups turn in Handout 4.4 and complete Handout 4.5: Student Reflection.

Going to the Store

Model your own store for the class. This can be done in several ways.

◆ Open a bakery or other type of store with real or fake items. Students can shop using currency provided (board game money, marbles, etc.). As they shop, you will keep a running tab of items purchased and provide students with receipts. Once the store is closed, you will count up the money and make sure you have a balanced register, showing the math involved.

◆ You could go online shopping and as a class buy various items, figuring out how much change would be provided. Once the class has finished shopping, count up the money and make sure you have a balanced register, showing the math involved.

You will also want to figure out how much the tax will be on items purchased. You should use the state sales tax to figure how much this would be. If you are working with advanced students, you could include discounts. You would need to show students how they figure out how much to take off based on the percentage off. Students will become more familiar with these concepts in upcoming lessons.

Balance is determined by the amount of items sold as compared to the amount of money in the register. Balance of the register should equal the dollar amount you started with plus the amount of dollars worth of merchandise sold. If you have more money in the register than you should, you have shorted a customer in giving back their change or charged them too much for their items. If you have less money in the register than you should, you have given the customer back more than you should have or did not charge them enough for their items. If you gave everyone the correct change and charged the correct amount, the register should reflect that by matching the sales receipts plus the amount of change you started with.

LESSON

Working With Decimals

Adding and Subtracting

Tell students: *When you are adding decimals you must always line up the decimal points. In other words, whether there are two numbers before the decimals or more, the decimal gets lined up and brought down to the sum total:*

$$58.90 + 73.047 = 131.947$$

The same concept applies when you are subtracting decimals:

$$9546.25 - 691.10 = 8855.15$$

Multiplying and Dividing

Tell students: *It is different when multiplying decimals. There are generally two rules when multiplying decimals: Multiply normally, ignoring the decimal points. You actually want to get the decimal point out of the way. Then put the decimal point in the answer—it will have as many decimal places as the two original numbers combined.*

$$58.9 \times 3.35 = 197.315$$

When you are dividing decimals you must turn the *divisor* (the number you're dividing by) into a whole number by moving the decimal point all of the way to the right; at the same time, move the decimal point in the *dividend* (the number you're dividing) the same number of places to the right.

$$23.5 \div \mathbf{1.25} = 2350 \div \mathbf{125} = 18.8$$

Calculating Sales Tax and Discounts

Tax

Tell students that sales tax is normally a percentage. It is calculated as a percentage of the price of a good or service and is added to the purchase price of those goods and services. Provide students with the sales tax rate for your state (refer to the state sales tax rates). For an up-to-date rate, refer to the interactive map located at http://www.tax-rates.org/taxtables/sales-tax-by-state.

Once you have done this you can figure out the sales tax by doing the following. An example would be Maine's state tax: 5.5%.

First, convert this to a decimal by moving it two spaces to the left:

$$.055$$

Second, multiply this percentage by the retail price of the item. This amount is the sales tax.

$$.055 \times \text{cost of a pencil } \$0.75 = .04$$

Third, add the sales tax to the price of the item to determine the total price of the purchase.

$$.75 + .04 = \$0.79 \text{ total}$$

Share some example problems with students, using different states and different item costs.

Lesson: Calculating Sales Tax and Discounts, *continued*

Discounts

Tell students: *Typically, when stores offer discounts it is done with a percentage. For example, take 10% off the cost or something in the clearance aisle that is marked down by 40%. How do you figure out how much you have saved? Just like the sales tax, the percentage needs to be turned into a decimal. This time, instead of adding the two numbers together, you subtract to get the discounted price.*

Share an example with a discount of 15%. First, convert to a decimal by moving it two spaces to the left:

$$15\% = .15$$

Second, multiply this percentage by the retail price of the item, $9.61. This amount is the discount off the original price.

$$.15 \times \$9.61 = 1.44$$

Third, subtract the discount from the price of the item to determine the total price of the purchase.

$$9.61 - 1.44 = \$8.17 \text{ total}$$

The discount is always pre-tax so tax would need to be figured out from the new price.

Share some example problems with students, using different discounts and different item costs.

HANDOUT 4.1

Decimals

Directions: Solve the following problems, using what you have learned about decimals.

1. Align the following numbers properly to be added:

    593.95   98.901   3013.4   402.4021   73.0   275.301

2. Add the decimals.
    a. $93.92 + 192.056 =$ c. $29 + 492.2 =$

    b. $72.4 + 8.345 =$ d. $6524.608 + 301.7 =$

3. Subtract the decimals.
    a. $520.8 - 8.936 =$ c. $3913.4720 - 201.97 =$

    b. $9310.67 - 777.0 =$ d. $63.06 - 9.492 =$

Handout 4.1: Decimals, *continued*

4. Multiply the decimals.

   a. $98.6 \times 3.56 =$

   c. $17.5 \times 5.96 =$

   b. $578.23 \times 12 =$

   d. $4758.36 \times 8.3 =$

5. Divide the decimals.

   a. $18.6 \div 3 =$

   c. $7.5 \div 5 =$

   b. $78.24 \div 12 =$

   d. $4758.36 \div 8 =$

HANDOUT 4.2

Sales Tax and Discounts

Directions: Answer the following questions using states' sales tax rates and your knowledge of calculating dicounts.

1. How much would a $449.82 TV cost in West Virginia?

2. How much would a $3.27 gallon of milk cost in South Dakota?

3. How much would a 99-cent bag of ice cost in Texas?

4. How much would a $15,983 car cost in Colorado?

5. How much would a $17.65 DVD cost in Missouri?

Handout 4.2: Sales Tax and Discounts, *continued*

6. How much is a 10% discount off an iPod that costs $133.04?

7. How much is a 30% discount off a dress that costs $27.88?

8. How much is a 15% discount off a refrigerator that costs $899.99?

9. How much is a 50% discount off a candy bar that costs $.75?

10. How much is a 8% discount off a house that costs $279,674?

Name: _____ Date: _____

Inventory Sheet

Qty.	Description	Unit Price	Total
		Total Value of Inventory	

Name: _____ Date: _____

HANDOUT 4.4

Invoice Sheet

Qty.	Description	Unit Price	Discount	Total
			Subtotal	
			Sales Tax	
			Total	
		Change That Register Began With		
		Total in Register Now		

HANDOUT 4.5

Student Reflection

Directions: As a group, answer the following questions, considering everyone's perspective.

1. What was successful about this project for you?

2. What is something you would change, and how would it have improved how things turned out?

3. How do you feel you worked as a group?

4. What was the most important thing you learned from this project?

PRODUCT RUBRIC

Playing Store

Overall	Store	Mathematics
Excellent (A)	• The invoice is filled out in detail, indicating everything that was sold, for how much, and how many. • Store looks professional with clearly marked prices and an organized set up that makes it easy for people to shop. • Five sales are offered and show a variety of different percentages.	• The discount from sales is calculated correctly for all items. • The tax for purchases is calculated correctly. • Register funds balance with the invoice perfectly, matching the inventory sold with the cash in the drawer.
Good (B–C)	• The invoice is filled out, indicating everything that was sold, for how much, and how many but lacks detail, making it difficult to understand clearly. • Store looks professional with clearly marked prices and an organized set up that makes it easy for people to shop. • Five sales are offered but show a limited variety of different percentages.	• The discount from sales is calculated correctly for most of the items but not all. • The tax for purchases is calculated correctly for most items but not all. • Although the register funds do not balance perfectly, the invoice is only $5 or less either above or below the inventory sold.
Needs Work (D–F)	• The invoice is filled but does not include everything that was sold, for how much, and/or how many. • Store does not look professional; prices are not indicated clearly and/or store is so unorganized that it makes it difficult to shop. • Less than five sales are offered or are all the same percent discount.	• The discount from sales is not calculated correctly, either giving too much of a discount or not enough. • The tax for purchases is not calculated correctly for many of the items. • The register funds do not balance perfectly, and the invoice is more than $5 either above or below the inventory sold.

5 Interview

Students often imagine teachers as the experts of their disciplines. If you are a language arts teacher, you are expected to be able to spell every single word in the English language correctly or to have read every book in the library. If you are a math teacher, you should know how to solve any math problem or know all of the mathematical principles that govern the discipline.

We as teachers know the truth: There are times when we simply do not know the answer, or we are teaching a topic we are not comfortable with. Having students interview an expert on a topic is a good learning tool that provides a real-world connection. Not only that, unlike using a book or the Internet to find an answer, the students can ask exactly what it is they want to know and receive an instant answer. There is no inferring or reading between the lines. It is a direct way to get content and insight about a topic.

What It Looks Like

Interviews can be done in a couple of ways. One way is for the student herself to locate an expert in a topic she wants to know more about and conduct an individual interview. The interview is tailored to this student's needs and she gains valuable information from the source.

A second way to conduct an interview is for the teacher to bring in an expert or panel of experts for the students to question. There does need to be a format to this process. You do not want to just turn students loose to ask any questions that come to mind. Students might ask off-topic questions or even inappropriate ones, and time that could have been spent getting valuable insight from the speaker is wasted. Bringing in an expert can take the learning to a deeper, more meaningful level.

Bridge Over Troubled Water

In this project, students will work in groups to build a bridge out of toothpicks, designing, buying the materials with their budget, and constructing a final product and seeing how much weight their structure can hold. They must also identify the different types of lines they use in their construction. They will conduct two interviews with an architect or engineer about the plans for their bridge and its construction.

Connections to CCSS

- 4.G.A.1

Materials

- Project Outline: Bridge Over Troubled Water (student copies)
- Suggested Timeline
- Lesson: History of Bridges
- Handout 5.1: Bridge-Building Rules (student copies)
- Handout 5.2: Bridge Materials (student copies)
- Handout 5.3: Balance Sheet (student copies)
- Handout 5.4: How to Conduct an Interview (student copies)
- Product Rubric (student copies)

Supplemental Materials

- An expert interviewee (engineer, architect)
- Bridge-building materials (cardboard, toothpicks)

PROJECT OUTLINE

Bridge Over Troubled Water

Directions: Humankind has been making bridges for thousands of years. As technology advances, so do the techniques we use to make bridges. There is a lot of math and science that goes into the construction of a bridge. Bridges are a series of intersecting, parallel, and perpendicular lines and line segments arranged to support heavy weights.

You and your group will build a bridge out of toothpicks, designing, buying the materials with your budget, and constructing a final product and seeing how much weight your structure can hold. You must also identify the different types of lines you use in your construction. You will conduct two interviews with an architect or engineer about the plans for your bridge and its construction.

Members of your group will take on the following roles:

- **Accountant:** Responsible for keeping balance sheets and writing checks to track expenses, staying under budget.
- **Architect:** Responsible for drawing the plans for the bridge from four different vantage points.
- **Foreman:** Responsible for the appearance and construction of the bridge, which must match the plans and be visually pleasing.
- **Safety Inspector:** Responsible for following building codes, making sure there are no violations.
- **Engineer:** Responsible for seeing how much weight the bridge can hold.

SUGGESTED TIMELINE

DAY				
1 Introduce the project and conduct Lesson: History of Bridges.	**2** Have students form groups and review Handout 5.1: Building Rules.	**3** Have groups begin planning their bridges (see Handout 5.2 and 5.3).	**4** Have groups continue planning their bridges.	**5** Distribute Handout 5.4 and review interview protocols.
6 Have groups prepare for the interview.	**7** Conduct an expert interview about bridge plans.	**8** Have groups revise their plans based on the interview.	**9** Have groups begin bridge construction.	**10** Have groups continue bridge construction.
11 Have groups continue bridge construction.	**12** Have groups complete bridge construction.	**13** Conduct an expert interview about bridge constructions.	**14** Have groups revise their constructions based on the interviews.	**15** Have groups present bridges, assessing them (see Product Rubric).

History of Bridges

Tell students that basic bridges evolved from natural bridges, such as fallen tree trunks, vines hanging over rivers, and large stones. The Ancient Romans refined bridges with two important contributions: arches (which support more weight than flat surfaces alone) and natural cement (which allowed them to build long bridges). Ancient China also contributed with its Great Stone Bridge, an open-spandrel arch bridge (a shallower arch than that of the Romans). Share with students images of examples of such bridges.

Leonardo da Vinci and Galileo furthered bridge technology, developing theories about the strength of building materials. Thus, bridge building became more exact, and the development of metal was a major advancement. The first cast-iron bridge was built in 1779 in England.

Share with students examples of bridges, including:
- arch bridges,
- suspension bridges,
- beam bridges,
- clapper bridges,
- floating pontoon bridges,
- truss bridges,
- cantilever bridges, and
- composite bridges.

HANDOUT 5.1

Bridge-Building Rules

Directions: You must follow these rules and codes while constructing your bridge. Failure to do so could result in fines and penalties.

- You have a budget of $2 million to spend. You cannot go over this.
- The bridge will be judged on the quality of building and the strength of the bridge.
- The bridge must be built according to code and using only the materials purchased at the Saw Lumber Company.

Bridge-Building Code

1. Bridge must be built on a piece of cardboard, 15 cm by 35 cm.

2. There must be a 15 cm-wide river in the middle of the cardboard.

3. Draw one 5 cm square at each end of the cardboard, 2.5 cm from the river and 2.5 cm from the edge.

4. Draw and cut a 4 cm square exactly in the center of the cardboard in the river. Only glue may be used to join the toothpicks.

5. The bridge must at all times touch only the cardboard inside the drawn squares.

6. The bridge must be more than 5 cm high. This distance is measured from the cardboard to where the deck of the bridge would be.

7. A 5 cm-tall boat must be able to travel the length of the river.

8. The bridge must be at least 4 cm wide.

9. A 3.5 cm-tall truck must be able to travel the length of the road.

Handout 5.1: Bridge-Building Rules, *continued*

Requirements for Plans

1. Plans must show four views: the view from each end, the side view, and the top view.

2. The plans must be legible and may not be changed once construction has begun.

3. Plans must have correctly labeled:
   - points,
   - lines,
   - line segments,
   - rays,
   - angles,
   - perpendicular lines, and
   - parallel lines.

Name: _____ Date: _____

HANDOUT 5.2

Bridge Materials

Directions: Use the following price list and the order form to select your materials.

Saw Lumber Company Warehouse Price List

- Land (cardboard) $500,000
- Lumber (toothpicks) $10,000 for wood (flat) $20,000 for steel (round)
- Cable (string) $500 per cm
- Welding Material (glue) $850 per day
- Building Plan Permit (4 sheets of graph paper) $40,000
- Extra Permits $10,000 per sheet
- Audit Service $2,000

Daily Order Form

Qty.	Description	Unit Price	Total

Name: _____ Date: _____

Handout 5.2: Bridge Materials, *continued*

Qty.	Description	Unit Price	Total
		Total Cost	

Name: _____ Date: _____

HANDOUT 5.3

Balance Sheet

Qty	Description	Day Item Ordered	Unit Price	Total
			Total	

Name: _____ Date: _____

How to Conduct an Interview

Directions: As part of this project, you will interview an engineer mentor, who will offer advice on your plans and then your model. The following steps will help you prepare and conduct your interview.

1. Know your stuff. The best way to generate interview questions is to know as much as you can. Create a list of 15 specific questions that can be answered with more than "yes" or "no." You want to get your interviewee talking.

2. Be polite when you contact your interviewee, and ask when a good time would be to do the interview. An in-person interview is ideal, but a phone interview is acceptable.

3. Come prepared with a pen or pencil, a notebook, a recording device, and your questions. Practice your questions in advance. If you plan to record your interview, be sure to ask permission.

4. Be professional:
   ◇ Arrive (or call) on time.
   ◇ Be polite and look your interviewee in the eye.
   ◇ Listen carefully; ask follow-up questions and for more information about things you don't understand.
   ◇ Act naturally. Although it is an interview, it should still feel like a conversation.

5. Even if you are recording, take notes. Don't try to write every word. Just take down the important things. After the interview, expand your notes with what you remember and by conducting more research. Highlight what you think are the most important points.

Note. Adapted from "How to Conduct a Journalistic Interview" by Scholastic News Kids Press Corps, n.d., retrieved from http://www.scholastic.com/teachers/article/how-conduct-journalistic-interview.

PRODUCT RUBRIC

Bridge Over Troubled Water

Overall	Accountant/ Bookkeeping	Plans	Model
Excellent (A)	◆ There are no rule violations and no fines had to be paid. ◆ Expenses are all accounted for and come in under budget. ◆ Balance sheet and order forms are consistently mathematically correct during the project.	◆ Plans correctly label all math concepts, including but not limited to points, lines, line segments, rays, angles, perpendicular lines, and parallel lines. ◆ Plans are neat and look professional, lines are straight, and parts are clearly labeled. ◆ Engineer mentor was consulted about the plans and adjustments were made based on the suggestions.	◆ Model of the bridge looks exactly like the plan. ◆ Adjustments were made based on the suggestions of the engineer mentor, which improved the construction. ◆ Building code was followed correctly without any violations.
Good (B–C)	◆ There are minor violations of rules and small fines had to be paid. ◆ Expenses are all accounted for but are over budget by less than $10,000. ◆ Balance sheet is mathematically correct and order forms mostly correct, but a couple had to be reworked.	◆ Plans correctly label all math concepts limited to only points, lines, line segments, rays, angles, perpendicular lines, and parallel lines. ◆ Plans are neat and look professional most of the time, but a few places could look nicer and/or are not consistently labeled. ◆ Engineer mentor was consulted about the plans, but very few adjustments were made based on the suggestions.	◆ Model of the bridge looks generally like the plan, but there are a couple of instances where they do not match. ◆ Adjustments were made based on the suggestions of your engineer mentor but did not necessarily improve the construction. ◆ Building code was mostly followed correctly with just some minor violations.

Name: _____ Date: _____

Product Rubric: Bridge Over Troubled Water, *continued*

Overall	Accountant/ Bookkeeping	Plans	Model
Needs Improvement (D–F)	♦ There are major violations of rules, thus large fines had to be paid. ♦ Expenses are not all accounted for and/or are over budget by more than $10,000. ♦ Balance sheet is not mathematically correct and/or many order forms were not correct and had to be reworked.	♦ Plans do not correctly label all math concepts, such as points, lines, line segments, rays, angles, perpendicular lines, and parallel lines. ♦ Plans are sloppy and do not look professional and/or nothing or very little is labeled. ♦ Engineer mentor was not consulted about the plans and/or no adjustments were made based on the suggestions.	♦ Model of the bridge looks almost nothing like the plan and/or has major differences. ♦ Engineer mentor was not consulted and/or adjustments were not made based on the suggestions. ♦ Building code was not always followed, resulting in some major violations.

6 Exhibition

An exhibition is just as it states: an exhibit of what the students have learned. An audience usually views the exhibition, whether it is made up of other students in the class, other classes from the school, parents, or outside audience members. The tricky thing about an exhibition is that the students cannot explain themselves orally; they must let the work explain itself. The analogy I often use with students when demonstrating an exhibition is the telling of a joke: "Two guys walk into a bar. The third one ducks." Nearly every time I tell this joke, I get puzzled looks and furrowed brows. I always feel a need to explain the joke: "You see, the bar in this case is not an establishment where one purchases alcohol. The bar is an actual metal bar that the people physically walk into . . ."

It's hilarious, right? Wrong. Because I have to explain the joke, it is not funny (no matter how much I think it is). Exhibitions are the exact same way. If you have to verbally explain the exhibit, the exhibit is not accomplishing what it is supposed to. When you go to an art exhibition, the artist is not there to explain what she did and why she did it. The piece has to stand on its own merits.

What It Looks Like

How a student approaches an exhibition is very different from other PBAs. Let us say for the sake of argument that a student creates a trifold as a product. If the student were using an oral presentation as this performance assessment, he might have a few meaningful visuals such as photos or graphs to enhance his explanation. He would not write out everything he plans to say on the board. Otherwise, he will feel compelled to read it verbatim and give a very stiff oral presentation. In an exhibition, the explanation would need to be written out because there is no one there to orally explain it.

An exhibition can come in many forms. A few common ones include:

- trifold,
- poster,
- PowerPoint presentation,
- short story/poem,
- video,
- piece of artwork or a craft, or
- photography series.

No matter which form a student chooses, first and foremost it must inform the audience and allow it to learn from the exhibition.

Coordinate Plane the Dots

In this project, students will work in groups to use coordinate planes to create their own connect-the-dot coloring book. They must provide coordinates, which others can use to find the dots and connect them to form a picture that can be colored. They should include 10 pages, create a theme for the book, and develop an answer key.

Connections to CCSS

- 5.G.A.1
- 5.G.A.2

Materials

- Project Outline: Coordinate Plane the Dots (student copies)
- Suggested Timeline
- Lesson: How to Use Coordinate Planes

- Lesson: Using Coordinate Planes in the Real World
- Handout 6.1: Determining Points on a Coordinate Plane (student copies)
- Handout 6.2: Plotting Continents (student copies)
- Product Rubric (student copies)

PROJECT OUTLINE

Coordinate Plane the Dots

Directions: Coordinate planes are determined by a horizontal number line, called the x-axis, and a vertical number line, called the y-axis, intersecting at a point called the origin. Each point in the coordinate plane is specified by an ordered pair of numbers.

In groups of five, you will use this mathematical function to create your own connect-the-dot coloring book. You must provide coordinates, which others can use to find the dots and connect them to form a picture that can be colored. You should include 10 pages (10 illustrations), create a theme for the book, and develop an answer key.

SUGGESTED TIMELINE

DAY				
1 Introduce the project and conduct Lesson: How to Use Coordinate Planes.	**2** Have students complete Handout 6.1: Determining Points on a Coordinate Plane.	**3** Conduct Lesson: Using Coordinate Planes in the Real World and distribute Handout 6.2.	**4** Have students form groups and determine a theme for their coloring books.	**5** Have students begin working on their coloring books.
6 Have students continue working on their coloring books.	**7** Have students continue working on their coloring books.	**8** Have students continue working on their coloring books.	**9** Have students complete their coloring books.	**10** Have students share their books with other groups, who will try to determine what the dots create (see Product Rubric).

LESSON

How to Use Coordinate Planes

Tell students that coordinate planes are how we plot points on a graph. In order to create a graph you need to have two lines; an x-axis and a y-axis. Display an example of a coordinate plane.

The x-axis runs horizontally. In the center of this line is zero. Anything to the right of zero is a positive number and anything to the left of zero is a negative number. The y-axis runs vertically. In the center of this line is zero. Anything above zero is a positive number and anything below zero is negative.

The x-axis lines and y-axis lines form an imaginary grid. Plotting a point on the grid, involves numbering coordinates. The x-axis is written first and the y-axis second. Depending on which quadrant a point lies in, its numbers will differ.

- Quadrant I is two positive numbers.
- Quadrant II is a positive x number and a negative y number.
- Quadrant III is two negative numbers.
- Quadrant IV is a negative x number and a positive y number.

Provide several examples of coordinates for students. Then, distribute Handout 6.1: Determining Points on a Coordinate Plane for students to complete.

Using Coordinate Planes in the Real World

Tell students that where they will most often see coordinate planes in the real world is the use of a GPS—a feature that most phones have. Using a satellite, this Global Positioning System takes into account the latitude and longitude lines on the globe. Display a world map with latitude and longitude lines. Tell students that much like the coordinate plane, these lines form a grid where a point can be given an absolute location. Latitude is the x-axis and longitude is the y-axis. And just like the coordinate plane created four quadrants, the latitude and longitude lines do the same.

Tell students: *We call these quadrants hemispheres. Using coordinates you should be able to pinpoint any spot on the planet. But instead of using positive or negatives, latitude is divided into west and east while longitude is divided into north and south. For instance, what continent would we be at under the following coordinates, 140 degrees east and 30 degrees south?* (Australia.)

Distribute Handout 6.2: Plotting Continents for students to complete.

HANDOUT 6.1

Determining Points on a Coordinate Plane

1.

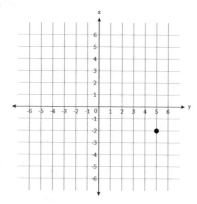

4.

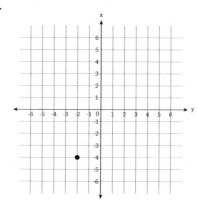

2.

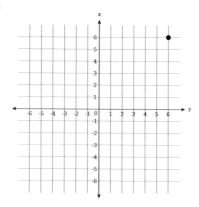

5.

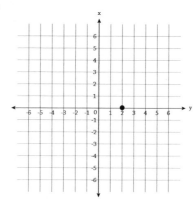

3.

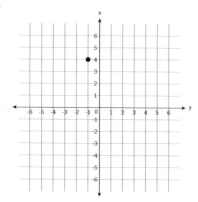

6.

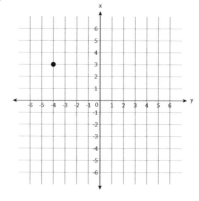

HANDOUT 6.2

Plotting Continents

Directions: Using the map, identify the continents found at the following coordinates.

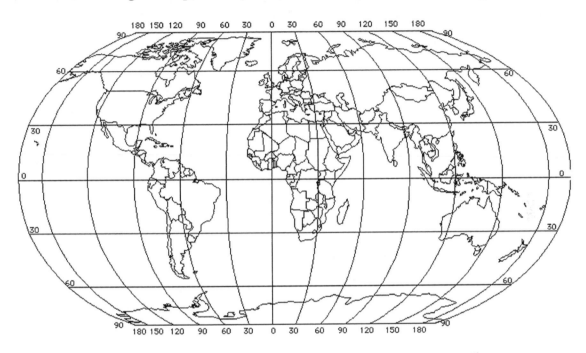

1. 20° E, 20° N

2. 110° E, 50° N

3. 100° W, 40° N

4. 10° E, 80° S

5. 140° W, 70° N

6. 20° E, 50° N

7. 60° W, 30° S

8. 40° E, 0°

9. 70° W, 50° S

10. 120° E, 20° S

Name: _____ Date: _____

PRODUCT RUBRIC

Coordinate Plane the Dots

Overall	Book	Math Concepts
Excellent (A)	◆ Coloring book has 10 different pages with complex coordinates. ◆ Book has an overall theme that all of the pages connect to. ◆ Pages are drawn professionally, and the book looks as though it could be purchased in a store.	◆ Graphing coordinates for all 10 pages are done clearly and correctly, making it easy for someone to complete the puzzle. ◆ Grid clearly shows the x- and y-axis, correctly numbering the grid in all four quadrants for all 10 puzzles. ◆ Answer key correctly graphs the points on the coordinate plan for all 10 puzzles, clearly showing the shape the coordinates create.
Good (B–C)	◆ Coloring book has 10 different pages with simple coordinates. ◆ Book has an overall theme that most the pages connect to but not all. ◆ Pages are drawn well, and the book looks like a high-quality student project.	◆ Graphing coordinates for all 10 pages are done correctly, although it is not always easy for someone to follow and complete the puzzle. ◆ Grid shows the x- and y-axis, but not all puzzles correctly number the grid in all four quadrants. ◆ Answer key correctly graphs the points on the coordinate plan for all 10 puzzles, but does not always clearly show the shape the coordinates create.
Needs Improvement (D–F)	◆ Coloring book has less than 10 different pages. ◆ Book does not have an overall theme, and the pages appear to be very random. ◆ Pages are drawn in a sloppy manner and do not reflect high-quality work.	◆ Graphing coordinates are not correct for all 10 pages and/or not well organized, making it difficult for someone to follow and complete the puzzle. ◆ Grid does not always shows the x- and y-axis and/or many of the puzzles incorrectly number the grid in all four quadrants. ◆ Answer key does not always correctly graph the points on the coordinate plane, failing to show the shape the coordinates create.

7 Essay

Essays are often thought of only for use in language arts class, but essays can be used for any subject area concerning any topic. An essay basically asks a student to explain what she has learned in written form. You would think this would simply be a translation of what the student is thinking into words, but that is easier said than done. Many students have difficulty making this translation, so it is important to teach writing in all subject areas so that students become familiar with how to make this translation.

What It Looks Like

Essays have a basic five-part structure:
- **Thesis statement:** This explains the purpose of the essay. It can be thought of as an introduction, but the thesis should be reiterated throughout the essay. It should be strong enough to be able to be backed up with three pieces of evidence.
- **Evidence 1**: This lays out the evidence that proves the thesis with supporting details. This might be an example from the text (language arts), an example problem (math or science), or a citation of a specific event that backs the thesis (social studies).
- **Evidence 2**: This is the same as Evidence 1, but with a second example.

- **Evidence 3:** This is the same as Evidence 1 and 2, but with a third example.
- **Conclusion:** This summarizes the main thesis and the arguments made. Lots of gifted students like to skip this step because they think they are just repeating themselves. It is safest to assume nothing about the reader and be as clear as possible.

Build a Fort

In this project, students will design the perfect fort. They will first design the fort on paper and then create a model, making sure they include accurate area and perimeter measurements. They will ensure the design is structurally sound and mathematically correct before building. They will then write an essay, discussing why they built the fort the way they did and explaining why they chose the sizes they did for area and perimeter.

Connections to CCSS

- 3.MD.D.8
- 4.MD.A.3

Materials

- Project Outline: Build a Fort (student copies)
- Suggested Timeline
- Lesson: How to Find Perimeter and Area
- Handout 7.1: Perimeter and Area (student copies)
- Handout 7.2: Structure of the Essay (student copies)
- Product Rubric (student copies)

PROJECT OUTLINE

Build a Fort

Directions: Haven't you ever wanted to make the ultimate fort in your backyard for you and your friends to meet in?

Here you will have the chance to design the perfect fort. You will first design the fort on paper and then create a model of the fort, making sure you include accurate area and perimeter measurements. Make sure the design is structurally sound and mathematically correct before building. You will then write an essay, discussing why you built the fort the way you did and explaining why you chose the sizes you did for area and perimeter.

1. Your fort must have at least two rooms to it so either it is a two-story fort or has two or more adjoining rooms.

2. Each room must be a rectangular shape but cannot be the exact same size. They must either have the same perimeter but different areas or the same area but different perimeters.

3. On your plans, you need to label both the perimeter and area of each room, presented as math problems (i.e., leave a missing side and explain how to find it in your essay).

SUGGESTED TIMELINE

DAY				
1 Introduce the project and share examples of forts.	**2** Conduct Lesson: How to Find Perimeter and Area.	**3** Have students complete Handout 7.1: Perimeter and Area.	**4** Review Handout 7.1., as well as the tips for drafting plans (see p. 107).	**5** Have students begin to plan their fort.
6 Have students continue to plan their fort.	**7** Have students continue to plan their fort.	**8** Have students continue to plan their fort.	**9** Have students check the math in their plan, making sure measurements and equations are correct.	**10** Have students create a list of supplies they will need to build their model.
11 Have students begin building the model of their fort.	**12** Have students continue building the model of their fort.	**13** Have students continue building the model of their fort.	**14** Have students continue building the model of their fort.	**15** Review the basic structure of an essay (see Handout 7.2).
16 Have students begin writing their essay.	**17** Have students continue writing their essay.	**18** Have students complete writing their essay.	**19** Have students turn in their plans, models, and essays (see Product Rubric).	

How to Find Perimeter and Area

Perimeter

Tell students that in order to figure out the perimeter of an object, they must simply add the total of all sides. For their forts, there will more than likely be four sides because they will be creating either a square or rectangle polygon.

Share with students several examples of rectangles and squares with different side lengths and how to calculate the perimeters.

Area

Ask students how they think they would find the area of an object. Rather than just finding out the distance around the outside of the shape, area involves the entire shape inside and outside. Tell students to think of the shape as made up of little squares. Consider a 5 x 5 square. If you count all of the squares, there are 25 of them, making the area 25. Rather than having to put squares in a shape every time, they can use a formula to determine area; $A = L \times W$. That formula is the length multiplied by the width of the shape.

Comparing Area and Perimeter

Tell students that it is possible to have two rectangles with the same perimeter and different areas or with the same area and different perimeters. For example, consider two rectangles that measure 7 x 6 ft and 9 x 4 ft. The perimeter of both shapes is 26 feet. But the areas are 42 ft^2 and 36 ft^2, respectively.

Other shapes may have the same area but different perimeters. For example, consider two rectangles that measure 8 x 3 ft and 12 x 2 ft. The areas for both are 24 ft^2, but the perimeters are 22 ft and 28 ft, respectively.

Distribute Handout 7.1: Perimeter and Area for students to complete.

HANDOUT 7.1

Perimeter and Area

Directions: Complete the following problems.

Fill in the missing measurements, and then determine the perimeter.

1.
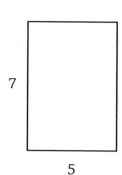
7
5

2.
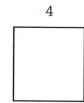
4

3.
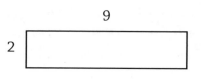
9
2

Using the perimeter, identify the missing measurements.

4.

5
P = 22

5.
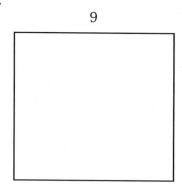
9
P = 34

6.

4
P = 24

Name: _____ Date: _____

Handout 7.1: Perimeter and Area, *continued*

Determine the area.

7.

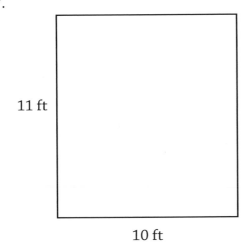

11 ft

10 ft

8.

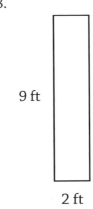

9 ft

2 ft

9.

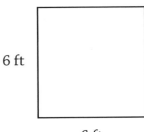

6 ft

6 ft

10. Draw and label two shapes that have the same perimeter but different areas.

11. Draw and label two shapes that have the same area but different perimeters.

HANDOUT 7.2

Structure of the Essay

Directions: This details the basic outline of your essay about your fort.

- **Thesis Statement:** This explains the purpose of the essay. It can be thought of as an introduction, but the thesis should be reiterated throughout the essay. The thesis statement for this project would address: How did you use perimeter and area in the planning and construction of your fort? In this section, you might want to describe why you created the fort the way you did.
- **Evidence 1:** This lays out the evidence that proves the thesis with supporting details. In this case, it should be what your perimeter is, how you arrived at that, and why you chose to make it the size you did.
- **Evidence 2:** This lays out the evidence that proves the thesis with supporting details. In this case, it should be what your area is, how you arrived at that, and why you chose to make it the size you did.
- **Evidence 3:** This lays out the evidence that proves the thesis with supporting details. In this case, it should be explaining your two rooms, exhibiting rectangles with the same perimeter and different areas or with the same area and different perimeters.
- **Conclusion:** This summarizes the main thesis and the arguments made. In addition, you need to make a judgment based on the evidence presented about why your fort is a good one. This judgment will need to be explained and supported.

Name: _____ Date: _____

PRODUCT RUBRIC

Build Your Own Fort

Overall	Essay	Plan	Model
Excellent (A)	◆ Essay includes a well-written introduction and conclusion that clearly state the purpose of the essay. ◆ Essay discusses in detail the shape, perimeter, and area of the fort, and why the decisions were made. ◆ Essay is grammatically correct with no spelling or punctuation errors or poor sentence structure.	◆ Plan clearly includes finding the perimeter given the side lengths, finding an unknown side length, and exhibiting rectangles with the same perimeter and different areas or with the same area and different perimeters. ◆ The area and perimeter formulas for rectangles in real-world and mathematical problems are displayed in plans with steps clearly demonstrated. ◆ Plans are neat and look professional, employing a ruler for straight lines and labeling aspects clearly.	◆ Model of the fort looks exactly like the plan. ◆ Model demonstrates a clear idea of how this fort would look like in real life. ◆ Model includes many details that bring it to life.
Good (B–C)	◆ Essay includes an introduction and conclusion that state the purpose of the essay but could be clearer with more explanation. ◆ Essay discusses the shape, perimeter, and area of the fort, and why the decisions were made the way they were, but there could be more detail to make it easier to understand. ◆ Essay is grammatically correct with just a few spelling or punctuation errors and/or awkward sentences.	◆ Plan includes finding the perimeter given the side lengths, finding an unknown side length, and exhibiting rectangles with the same perimeter and different areas or with the same area and different perimeters, but is not clearly laid out. ◆ The area and perimeter formulas for rectangles in real-world and mathematical problems are displayed in plans, but a few steps are not clearly demonstrated. ◆ Plans are neat and look professional most of the time, but a few places could look nicer and/or are not consistently labeled.	◆ Model of the fort looks generally like the plan, but there are a couple of instances where they do not match. ◆ Model demonstrates a general idea of how this fort would look in real life, but some parts are not as clear as they could be. ◆ Model includes a few details that bring it to life but missed opportunities to include others.

Product Rubric: Build Your Own Fort, *continued*

Overall	Essay	Plan	Model
Needs Work (D–F)	• Essay either does not include an introduction and/or conclusion, or it does not state the purpose of the essay very clearly. • Essay does not discuss either the shape, perimeter, and/or area of the fort and why the decisions were made the way they were. • Essay has many grammatical errors, such as spelling, punctuation, or sentence structure, making it difficult to read.	• Plan does not include either finding the perimeter given the side lengths, finding an unknown side length, or exhibiting rectangles with the same perimeter and different areas or with the same area and different perimeters. • The area and perimeter formulas for rectangles in real-world and mathematical problems are not displayed in plans and/or many steps.	• Model of the fort looks almost nothing like the plan and/or has major differences. • Model does not demonstrate how this fort would look in real life, making it difficult to figure out what this will look like. • Model includes little to no details, making for a bland fort that doesn't look like it would be that much fun to play in.

8 Research Paper

One way to look at a research paper is as an expanded essay. Essentially, it follows the same structure: introduction of thesis, evidence, and conclusion. The big difference is that students are also responsible for conducting independent research. For an essay, the teacher often provides the background information or data for a student to be able to answer the question presented in an essay format. The students are merely synthesizing what they have learned from the teacher and communicating how it fits into the essay. The essay can be written on the spot and is a culmination of what has been taught. A research paper, on the other hand, has the students acquiring the information for themselves by using various sources, including books, the Internet, or interviews. The writing aspect is the last thing the student will be doing. There is the process of finding, evaluating, and organizing the information. Finally, the student must properly cite sources.

What It Looks Like

The key to a good research paper is providing an outline for students to follow. The outline can be very basic or it can be detailed depending on the level of the student. The outline should walk students through what is expected in the paper. Students should be able to use this as a blueprint to construct their research paper.

It is important for students to understand there is a structure to a research paper and that the outline is the backbone upon which they will build the research. Once they understand this and have a solid outline, the creation of the paper becomes a matter of building it around the outline. This will make the writing of all future research papers easier.

Math in Real Life

In this project, students will write a research paper, identifying instances in real life where they might find a specific math concept. They will explain the math concept in a real-world situation, identify times in their own life when they might use it, and research a career where they might be called upon to continually use the math concept.

Connections to CCSS

+ 3.NBT.A.3
+ 4.NBT.A.3
+ 5.NBT.A.2

Materials

+ Project Outline: Math in Real Life (student copies)
+ Suggested Timeline
+ Lesson: Math in Real Life
+ Lesson: Conducting Research
+ Handout 8.1: Internet Scavenger Hunt (student copies)
+ Handout 8.2: Researching Your Topic (student copies)
+ Handout 8.3: Guidelines for Rough Draft (student copies)
+ Handout 8.4: Revising Your Draft (student copies)
+ Product Rubric (student copies)

Supplemental Materials

+ *Math Curse* by Jon Scieszka and Lane Smith (teacher's copy)

PROJECT OUTLINE

Math in Real Life

Directions: Have you ever been in math class and thought, "Why do I need to learn this?" or "When will I ever use this in my life?" Now is your time to find out.

You will write a research paper identifying places in real life where you might find a specific math concept. You will explain the math concept in a real-world situation, identify times in your own life when you might use it, and research a career where you might be called upon to continually use this math concept.

There should be five sections to your paper:

1. Introduction
   ◇ What is the math concept you are learning about?
   ◇ Do you think it might be an important concept to learn about it?
   ◇ Can you give an example of using this math concept in the classroom?

2. Explain math concept in real life
   ◇ Are there daily instances where someone would use this type of math?
   ◇ Give a specific problem someone might encounter in everyday life that would use this concept.
   ◇ Why might it be important for someone to understand this math concept?

3. Math in your life
   ◇ What are some ways you might use this math in your own life?
   ◇ Could you provide a scenario in which this math concept is used?
   ◇ How might your life be easier if you understood this math concept really well?

4. Math in a job
   ◇ In what jobs would you use this sort of math?
   ◇ Would you be interested in doing a job like this? Why or why not?
   ◇ How difficult would this job be for someone who did not understand this math concept?

5. Conclusion
   ◇ Now that you have researched it, do you feel different about the importance of this math concept?
   ◇ How might you see yourself using this math concept in the future?
   ◇ Do you think having a better understanding of this math concept will make your life easier? What are the advantages you see with this?

SUGGESTED TIMELINE

DAY				
1 Introduce the project and conduct Lesson: Math in Real Life.	**2** Either have students decide on a math concept to cover or assign one.	**3** Have students work on understanding the math concept.	**4** Have students work on understanding the math concept.	**5** Conduct conferences with students to make sure they understand their concept.
6 Conduct Lesson: Conducting Research (see Handout 8.1, Handout 8.2).	**7** Have students conduct research on their concept.	**8** Have students conduct research on their concept.	**9** Have students conduct research on their concept.	**10** Have students conduct research on their concept.
11 Have students conduct research on their concept.	**12** Students need to begin the rough draft of their paper (see Handout 8.3).	**13** Students need to continue the rough draft of their paper.	**14** Students need to continue the rough draft of their paper.	**15** Students need to finish the rough draft of their paper.
16 Have students revise their rough draft (see Handout 8.4).	**17** Students need to begin the final draft of their paper.	**18** Students need to continue the final draft of their paper.	**19** Students need to continue the final draft of their paper.	**20** Students need to finish the final draft of their paper (see Product Rubric).

Math in Real Life

Read to the class *Math Curse* by Jon Scieszka and Lane Smith. Use it to spark a discussion about how much math we encounter in everyday life.

Possible topics include:

- the different measurements in cooking,
- the numbers of people getting on and off the bus,
- the arrangement of students in a classroom,
- fractions for pizza slices,
- statistics in sports,
- the binary code in your computer or iPhone,
- anytime you buy something with money,
- figuring out the time and estimations of how much you have to do something,
- length of roads and trips, or
- dividing objects amongst groups of people.

LESSON

Conducting Research

Tell students that they can find almost anything on the Internet, which means they will always have to go through a lot of information that might not be relevant to their topic.

There are various search engines to help them find information, such as:

* Google (http://www.google.com),
* Yahoo (http://www.yahoo.com), and
* Bing (http://www.bing.com).

When they search, they will want to:

* be as specific as possible without being too specific (e.g., too general = "airplanes," too specific = "paper airplanes with cool decals");
* narrow their search without eliminating sites because they do not contain the exact wording; and
* not just use the first website they encounter (i.e., just because it comes up in a search does not mean it is what they are looking for).

Distribute Handout 8.1: Internet Scavenger Hunt. Tell students to imagine they are writing a report about oceans. If they Google the term "ocean," they retrieve more than 685,000,000 results. That's more than anyone can possibly go through. How do they refine their search? The scavenger hunt will show them how.

Have students select their research topics and distribute Handout 8.2: Researching Your Topic.

HANDOUT 8.1

Internet Scavenger Hunt

Directions: Use a search engine to answer the following questions.

1. How many hits do you get when you put in the search term "oceans"?

2. How many hits do you receive when you refine your search to "large oceans"?

3. How many hits do you receive when you refine your search to "large oceans western hemisphere"?

4. If you are trying to find out how many oceans there are, what key term could you use to refine your search even more?

5. Using one of the three search engines, determine what is the largest ocean.

6. How many oceans do we have on the planet Earth?

7. What is the definition of an ocean?

8. What is the oldest ocean and how old is it?

9. Go to the ORCA website at http://www.teamorca.org. Under "What we do" in the top menu, go to "Overview." What is ORCA's three-word mission?

10. Go to the NOAA website at http://www.noaa.gov. Go to "About our agency" and select the tab that says "NOAA in your state." How many pages of information are there under Alaska?

HANDOUT 8.2

Researching Your Topic

Directions: When you are conducting research, you should consider the following five steps.

Step 1: Construct Research Questions

Start by writing specific research questions. Doing so will help you narrow your topic and determine exactly what information you need. Sample questions:

- What is an ocean?
- What creates an ocean?
- How many oceans are there?
- What are the major oceans?
- How much space do the oceans take up on the planet?
- Are there other planets that we know of that have oceans?
- How many creatures live in the ocean?

Step 2: Figure Out Possible Sources of Information

Before going online, try to identify any sources that might have information on your topic. For example, you might list:

- National Geographic
- Oceanographers website
- Cousteau Society
- ORCA (Ocean Research and Conservation Association)
- NOAA (National Oceanic and Atmospheric Administration)
- Universities with a strong oceanic research focus

Step 3: Identify Keywords

Review the questions and sources you brainstormed in Steps 1–2, and circle the keywords. What is it specifically you want to find? Use this to refine your search.

Handout 8.2: Researching Your Topic, *continued*

Step 4: Get Ready to Search

You're finally ready to choose a tool(s) and begin your search. Depending on the time you have and your own personal preference, you can start with a search engine, or a specific site of your own choice.

If you are using a search engine, you will want to: Use the keywords you identified in Step 3 to develop your search query. The trick is to try several combinations of keywords. Remember—there's no one *right* way to conduct research online. Just be sure to start with a strategy and experiment with different search tools to get the best results.

Step 5: Finding Easy to Understand, School Appropriate Sites

Adding a simple suffix to your search may result in more student-appropriate, student-friendly results. For instance, refine your search to add the following:

- ... for kids
- ... for students
- ... for children
- ... for school

These will make the hits you receive from your search more age appropriate and easier to understand because you will be the audience they are written for.

HANDOUT 8.3

Guidelines for Rough Draft

Directions: Use the following guidelines as you write your rough draft.

1. Write legibly or type.

2. Skip lines.

3. Use one side of the paper.

4. Make sure you are following the outline in order.

5. Do not worry about spelling mistakes as much in the rough draft, but these will need to be corrected for the final draft.

6. Be sure you are answering the questions in the outline in detail.

7. Include lots of examples and evidence to further strengthen your point.

8. Turn the question into a statement as the beginning topic sentence.

9. Make sure there are clear transition sentences whenever the topic changes or a new paragraph begins.

10. Do not copy down sentences from your research word for word or cut and paste text from another source. This is called plagiarism.

11. You can use quotes, but they should not be longer than a single sentence.

12. There is no page limit, but it should be a well-developed paper. That means if you have really short paragraphs, you probably have not explained yourself very clearly or thoroughly.

HANDOUT 8.4

Revising Your Draft

Directions: Edit your paper for correct grammar, spelling, sentence structure, and content, using the following tips.

1. **First Round of Editing:** Using Handout 8.2, make sure everything is discussed and answered in detail. Read your paper, pretending you know nothing about your topic and this paper is teaching you everything you need to know about it.

2. **Second Round of Editing:** Using spell check is not always enough. You need to go through the paper and make sure things are spelled correctly and that the correct forms of words are used.

3. **Third Round of Editing:** During this round you will want to find a place where you can read the paper out loud. This is a good way to check that your sentence structure is clear and that what you are writing makes sense. If you have trouble saying a sentence out loud, chances are a person reading it will also struggle. Fix these awkward sentences so that your paper makes sense and flows.

4. **Final Round of Editing:** Use the rubric as a checklist to make sure you have met all of the requirements of the research paper and that it is of the quality level you want it to be. If there are sections that need improvement, what can be changed to get them into the excellent range?

PRODUCT RUBRIC

Math in Real Life

Overall	Outline	Math Content	Mechanics
Excellent (A)	• Paper follows the outline, making it easy to follow. • Student provides plenty of examples to back up statements made in the paper. • Student provides much detail, explaining concepts and ideas so that the reader can gain a full understanding of what is being discussed.	• Research is consistently paraphrased. • Math concept is explained with much detail, showing understanding. • Job is discussed in detail and there is a clear link between it and its use of the math concept.	• Paper has little to no spelling/grammatical errors. • Paper is typed in the correct format. • Sentence structure makes the paragraphs flow and easy to read.
Good (B–C)	• Paper follows the outline, but is not always easy to follow. • Student does not consistently provide examples. • Student provides detail, explaining concepts and ideas so that the reader can gain an understanding of what is being discussed, but could be clearer.	• Research is not always paraphrased. • Math concept is explained, showing basic understanding, but lack of details and/or examples does not show a depth of understanding. • Job is discussed and there is a link between it and its use of the math concept, but the link is not explained clearly enough.	• Paper has occasional spelling/grammatical errors, making more than a handful of mistakes. • Paper is typed but not always in the correct format. • Sentence structure flows and is easy to read for the most part, but has the occasional awkward sentence that causes confusion.
Needs Improvement (D–F)	• Paper does not follow the outline, causing the reader confusion. • Student provides little to no examples to back up statements. • Student does not provide much detail, leaving the reader confused about what is being discussed.	• Research is many times not paraphrased, but is taken word for word. • Math concept is not explained very well, leaving one to wonder if the student understands the concept. • Either the job researched does not really use math very much or there is no link at all between the job and the math concept.	• Paper has many spelling/grammatical errors, making it difficult to read at times. • Paper is typed in a sloppy manner, making it difficult to read. • Sentence structure is sloppy and difficult to follow.

9 Journal/ Student Log

Journals and student logs allow for a more informal style of writing. Although it is important for students to be able to write a proper essay, it is also important to give students the opportunity to be creative and not be constrained by the structure of an essay. Journals and student logs allow students to explore ideas without being tied to an essay format. The format need not even include complete sentences. Students can draw, write poetry, make lists, write letters from the perspective of another person, draw charts, or use any other form of expression.

Journals also do not need to be exclusive to language arts class. Students can journal in science, social studies, math, and even gym class. Journals show the progression of learning. Students can go back and see how much they have learned and what route they took to get there.

What It Looks Like

The nice thing about journal entries is that unlike an essay or research paper, which has a clear structure, there is more flexibility to look like whatever the teacher or student wishes for it to be. Journal entries usually start with a prompt. Writing prompts using higher level language allow for higher level thinking. It is important not to encourage lower level journal entries by assigning lower level prompts. Using key words from Bloom's taxonomy to do this will help in the writing of these higher level prompts (Sedita, 2012).

The Theory of Flight

In this project, students will be divided into groups of five and design and construct paper airplanes and fly them to see which of the designs is the most aerodynamic. Through trial and error, they will record the flights and compare them with others. They will compare and contrast their results, recording their results and experiences through 10 log entries.

Connections to CCSS

- 3.MD.B.4
- 4.MD.A.1

Materials

- Project Outline: The Theory of Flight (student copies)
- Suggested Timeline
- Lesson: Setting Up an Experiment
- Lesson: Using the Scientific Method
- Lesson: Converting Distances
- Lesson: Analyzing Data
- Handout 9.1: Log Entry Prompts (student copies)
- Handout 9.2: Which Plane Will Fly the Farthest? (student copies)
- Handout 9.3: Conversions (student copies)
- Handout 9.4: Plane Design Data (student copies)
- Product Rubric (student copies)

PROJECT OUTLINE

The Theory of Flight

Directions: Making paper planes is complicated. What makes one plane fly farther than another? What about the different designs makes one a better plane than another?

You and your group will design and construct paper airplanes and fly them to see which of the designs is the most aerodynamic. Through an experiment of trial and error, you will record the flights of these planes and compare them with others. You may determine which design is the most successful or create your own design and contest it against the others. Compare and contrast your results, recording your results and experiences through 10 log entries.

Each team member will be responsible for a different part of the experiment, but each must maintain his or her own log entries:

- **Pilot:** Responsible for flying the planes.
- **Engineer:** Responsible for making the planes.
- **Surveyor:** Responsible for measuring the distance of the planes.
- **Statistician:** Responsible for taking the data and converting it.
- **Analyst:** Responsible for taking data and putting it into charts.

SUGGESTED TIMELINE

DAY				
1 Introduce the project and distribute Handout 9.1. Conduct Lesson: Setting Up an Experiment, and distribute Handout 9.2 (Entry 1).	**2** Conduct Lesson: Using the Scientific Method. Have students form teams and set up their experiment (Entry 2).	**3** Have teams do background research, determine the five planes they will use, and make a hypothesis (Entry 3).	**4** Have teams construct their airplanes (Entry 4).	**5** Conduct Lesson: Converting Distances (see Handout 9.3). Have teams conduct their experiment, converting the distance of Flight 2 into meters (Entry 5).
6 Lesson on converting meters to cm, mm, and km. Have teams convert the distances the planes flew from centimeters to millimeters (Entry 6).	**7** Have teams convert the distances the planes flew from centimeters to kilometers (Entry 7).	**8** Conduct Lesson: Analyzing Data. Have teams show the distances flown in feet and inches on a line plot (Entry 8).	**9** Have teams analyze the data and record measurement equivalents in a table (Entry 9).	**10** Teams will report out their findings, using the data to support the conclusion and compare it to their hypothesis (Entry 10; see Product Rubric).

LESSON

Setting Up an Experiment

Create three paper airplanes, using different designs (myriad options are available online). Present them to the class, having students guess which plane they think will fly the farthest. Distribute Handout 9.2: Which Plane Will Fly the Farthest? for students to record their observations. Use the following questions to spark discussion about the experiment. Ask:

- Which do you think will fly the farthest?
- Which unit of measure would be best to figure out how far each plane will fly— kilometers, meters, centimeters, or millimeters? Why?
- Why did you pick the plane you did?
- Would it be more valid just to fly each plane once or multiple times? Why did you choose the one you did?
- What could affect the outcome of the experiment?
- Were you correct in your hypothesis? Why do you think the plane that went the furthest did so?

Explain to students that they will be running a similar experiment in groups where they will create and fly five planes, testing their hypothesis of which they believe will go the farthest. They will use the scientific method to conduct the experiment, and their end product will be a journal and recorded data in various units of measurement.

Using the Scientific Method

Tell students that there are six steps to the scientific method, each of which has to be taken into consideration when running a legitimate experiment. In order to make a legitimate experiment, it has to be repeatable. In other words, if someone ran through the exact same steps that they did, would they come up with the same results?

1. **Ask a question.** Which plane will fly the furthest?

2. **Do background research.** This can be anything from referencing past experiences, to asking people what they think, to actually conducting internet research and see what has happened to others. It can simply be a gut reaction or feeling but they need to be able to back up their reasoning with a thorough explanation in Step 3. Part of this will be researching different plane designs and deciding which one they want to use for the experiment.

3. **Construct a hypothesis.** In other words, what do you think will be the outcome of the experiment? What leads you to believe this (this is where your background research can be used)?

4. **Test the hypothesis by doing an experiment.** This is where students will conduct their measurements of which of the three designs they chose flew the farthest consistently. They will conduct a series of experiments to minimize the amount of variables that could affect the experiment.

5. **Analyze the data.** For this experiment, students are going to show measurement results by making a line plot, where the horizontal scale is marked off in appropriate units—whole numbers, halves, or quarters. Once they have done this, they will analyze the results and draw a conclusion.

6. **Report your results.** Students will develop a reflection where they look back on the results and think about how they might have been successful or different depending on certain variables.

Lesson: Using the Scientific Method, *continued*

What Is a Variable?

Variables are conditions that can affect the outcome of an experiment. Good scientists try to eliminate as many variables as possible from their experiments so that they are getting the most accurate results. Tell students: *An example of a variable could be the thickness of the paper you use to build your planes. In other words, if you use standard copy paper for one design but use cardstock for another, the difference in sturdiness and weight could have an effect on the outcome. To eliminate this variable, you would want to make the paper airplanes with the same thickness of paper. What are some other examples of possible variables?*

Possible answers:

- The same person doesn't throw all planes.
- The person throwing the planes throws some harder than others.
- The person doesn't use the same throwing technique with all of the planes.
- The person gets tired halfway through the experiment.
- Some planes are thrown indoors and others outdoors.
- One plane is made better than another.
- One plane has its folds taped down while another does not.
- You use different measuring tools to measure the distance.
- You are not accurate in your measurement.
- You lose half of your data and have to do that part of the experiment again.

LESSON

Converting Distances

Converting Feet and Inches to Meters

Tell students converting feet to meters involves a simple formula. It is easiest to first convert the feet to a total of inches. The formula for that is 1 foot = 12 inches. Then the formula for converting inches to meters would be 39.37007874 inches = 1 meter.

Converting Meters To Centimeters/Millimeters/Kilometers

Within the metric system, converting to different forms of measurement is usually just a movement of the decimal point rather than any complicated conversion:

$$1 \text{ meter} = 100 \text{ centimeters}$$
$$1 \text{ centimeter} = 10 \text{ millimeters}$$
$$1 \text{ kilometer} = 1{,}000 \text{ meters}$$

LESSON

Analyzing Data

Displaying Data on a Line Plot

For their eighth journal entry, students will need to display data on a line plot. Share with students the following steps:

1. **Gather your data:** In this case, you have already done this during your experiment.

2. **Organize your data:** The factors for your organization should be the type of plane and the number of the flight.

3. **Create a horizontal line.** Mark distance measurements in equal increments.

4. **Record data.** Make a mark above the horizontal line every time the data occurs. For example:

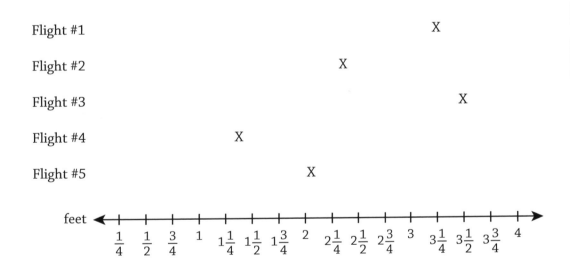

5. Interpret the data. In the example above, Flight 3 flew the farthest and Flight 4 was the shortest.

HANDOUT 9.1

Log Entry Prompts

Directions: Use the following prompts to write your log entries.

- **Entry 1:** Which plane did you think was going to fly the farthest in the teacher demonstration? Why did you think this was the case? Why do you think you were correct in your hypothesis or incorrect?

- **Entry 2:** Why do you think the scientific method is a good means of conducting an experiment? What would be advantages to using it? What would be disadvantages?

- **Entry 3**: Which designs did your team choose and why? Which one do you believe will fly the farthest and what leads you to believe this? Did the team agree with this or did they choose a different design?

- **Entry 4:** After constructing your five planes, do you still believe the hypothesis your team chose is the correct one? What leads you to support this or change your mind?

- **Entry 5:** What are five common, everyday objects you would measure using meters? Why would you use meters and not another unit of measurement?

- **Entry 6:** What are five common, everyday objects you would measure using centimeters? How about millimeters? Why would you use these units of measurement for those items and not another unit of measurement?

- **Entry 7:** Even though your team had to convert the measurements to kilometers, you usually wouldn't use this measurement for such short distances. What are five things you would you measure using kilometers and why?

- **Entry 8:** Show your measurement results by making a line plot, where the horizontal scale is marked off in appropriate units—whole numbers, halves, or quarters.

- **Entry 9:** Show your measurement results by recording measurement equivalents in a table (see Handout 9.4).

- **Entry 10:** After conducting your experiment, was your hypothesis correct? Why did you think it was or was not?

- **Reflection:** Do you think you would get the exact same results if you conducted the experiment again? Why or why not? What variables might affect the outcome of the experiment? What could you do in order to help get the same results in an experiment? What do you think is the most important thing you learned from running this experiment? How will you be able to use what you learned to do better on the next experiment?

Name: _____ Date: _____

HANDOUT 9.2

Which Plane Will Fly the Farthest?

Directions: Use this graphic organizer to record the results of your experiment.

1. Which plane do you think will fly the farthest? Circle one.
   a. Plane 1
   b. Plane 2
   c. Plane 3

   Why do you think it will fly farther than the others?

2. Record the distances the planes flew in the chart below.

	Plane 1	**Plane 2**	**Plane 3**
Flight 1			
Flight 2			
Flight 3			

Was your hypothesis correct?

HANDOUT 9.3

Conversions

Directions: Calculate the following conversions.

1. 5 ft 3 in = _____ in

2. 17 ft 11 in = _____ in

3. 9 ft 7 in = _____ in

4. 25 ft 1 in = _____ in

5. 231 in = _____ m

6. 72 in = _____ m

7. 29 in = _____ m

8. 521 in = _____ m

9. 5.8674 m =

    a. _____ cm

    b. _____ mm

    c. _____ km

10. 1.8288 m =

    a. _____ cm

    b. _____ mm

    c. _____ km

11. 0.7366 m =

    a. _____ cm

    b. _____ mm

    c. _____ km

12. 13.2334 m =

    a. _____ cm

    b. _____ mm

    c. _____ km

HANDOUT 9.4

Plane Design Data

Directions: Use this handout to record data as you test each of your planes.

Plane Design 1

Flight	Distance in Feet and Inches	Conversion
1		None.
2		m
3		cm
4		mm
5		km

Plane Design 2

Flight	Distance in Feet and Inches	Conversion
1		None.
2		m
3		cm
4		mm
5		km

Name: _____ Date: _____

Handout 9.4: Plane Design Data, *continued*

Plane Design 3

Flight	Distance in Feet and Inches	Conversion
1		None.
2		m
3		cm
4		mm
5		km

Plane Design 4

Flight	Distance in Feet and Inches	Conversion
1		None.
2		m
3		cm
4		mm
5		km

Plane Design 5

Flight	Distance in Feet and Inches	Conversion
1		None.
2		m
3		cm
4		mm
5		km

Name: _____   Date: _____

PRODUCT RUBRIC

Theory of Flight

Overall	Measurement	Data Display	Journal
Excellent (A)	◆ All measurements and conversions are correct.	◆ Student displays data on a line plot, where the scale is labeled with appropriate units, including halves and quarters. ◆ Student records equivalents in a table that is clearly labeled and easy to understand.	◆ Journal has 10 detailed entries that clearly show how the experiment was conducted and the thoughts and feelings of the experimenter. ◆ Journal includes a thoughtful reflection that provides additional insight to the experiment and what the student learned.
Good (B–C)	◆ Measurements and conversions are correct for the most part, but there are several mistakes.	◆ Student displays data on a line plot, where the scale is labeled, but not always with appropriate units, including halves and quarters. ◆ Student records equivalents in a table that is labeled but not always easy to understand.	◆ Journal has 10 entries that show how the experiment was conducted and the thoughts and feelings of the experimenter, but they lack some detail. ◆ Journal includes a reflection that provides additional insight to the experiment, but could include more insight.
Needs Work (D–F)	◆ Measurements and conversions have many mistakes.	◆ Student displays data on a line plot, but the scale is not labeled with appropriate units, including halves and quarters. ◆ Student records equivalents in a table that is not labeled or not easy to understand.	◆ Journal has less than 10 entries showing how the experiment was conducted and/or lacks detail of the thoughts and feelings of the experimenter. ◆ Journal either does not include a reflection or it adds little to no insight into what the student learned from the process.

10 Portfolio

A student portfolio is a collection of materials that represents what a student learned. It may be something as simple as a folder containing the student's best work, along with the student's evaluation of this work. It may also be articles or work from other sources that the student has commented or reflected on. The length of the portfolio is determined by the teacher. The portfolio could be a snapshot of what the student learned during a brief one-week project, or it can be an ongoing evolution of how that student has improved over the course of an entire year. For instance, the first part of a portfolio might contain an essay the student wrote on the first day of class. The remaining content of the portfolio might show work 6 weeks in, 12 weeks in, or at the semester break. What can be seen throughout this process is how the student has improved and acquired new skills or knowledge. Conceivably, a portfolio could track the student's progress for an entire year and even longer. The assessment of a portfolio comes more from the student commentary than it does from the pieces she selected as part of the portfolio. This commentary can be as informal as a student jotting down an observation from a highlighted piece of text to a formal essay that sums up the entire project or semester. Either one of these can be used in the classroom as a performance-based assessment.

What It Looks Like

According to Melissa Kelly (2014), there are three main factors that go into the development of a student portfolio assessment:

First, you must decide the purpose of your portfolio. For example, the portfolios might be used to show student growth, to identify weak spots in student work, and/or to evaluate your own teaching methods.

After deciding the purpose of the portfolio, you will need to determine how you are going to grade it. In other words, what would a student need in her portfolio for it to be considered a success and for her to earn a passing grade?

What should be included in the portfolio? Are you going to have students put of all of their work or only certain assignments? Who gets to choose? (para. 9)

You Are What You Eat

In this project, students will track their calorie intake for 3 weeks. They will choose two other nutritional aspects to track as well. At the end of the 3 weeks, they will write an analysis of their food habits, what they eat that is low or high in calories and other patterns that they notice. They will need to display their calorie intake on a scaled picture graph and a bar graph.

Connections to CCSS

+ 3.MD.B.3

Materials

+ Project Outline: You Are What You Eat (student copies)
+ Suggested Timeline
+ Lesson: How to Track Calories
+ Lesson: How to Create Graphs

- Handout 10.1: Using Graphs (student copies)
- Handout 10.2: Student Reflection (student copies)
- Product Rubric (student copies)

PROJECT OUTLINE

You Are What You Eat

Directions: Calorie tracking has become general practice among those trying to live a healthy lifestyle. Tracking calories and other nutritional aspects is a chance to use some math skills.

You will record what you eat and the amount of calories for a period of 3 weeks. You will choose two other nutritional aspects to track as well. At the end of the 3 weeks, you will write an analysis of your food habits, what you eat that is low or high in calories and other patterns that you notice. You will need to display your calorie intake on a scaled picture graph and a bar graph, as well as create several one- and two-step "how many more" and "how many fewer" questions, using information presented in your bar graph. You will collect all of this in a portfolio.

SUGGESTED TIMELINE

DAY				
1 Introduce project and conduct Lesson: How to Track Calories. Students should record Day 1 calories.	**2** Conduct Lesson: How to Create Graphs. Students should record Day 2 calories.	**3** Students should record Day 3 calories.	**4** Students should record Day 4 calories.	**5** Students should record Day 5 calories.
6 Students should record Days 6–7 calories (from the weekend, if applicaple) and Day 8 calories.	**7** Students should record Day 9 calories.	**8** Students should record Day 10 calories.	**9** Students should record Day 11 calories.	**10** Students should record Day 12 calories.
11 Students should record Days 13–14 calories (from the weekend, if applicaple) and Day 15 calories.	**12** Students should record Day 16 calories.	**13** Students should record Day 17 calories.	**14** Students should record Day 18 calories.	**15** Students should record Day 19 calories.
16 Students should record Days 20–21 calories (from the weekend, if applicaple). Have students begin organizing portfolios.	**17** Students should summarize their findings and draw conclusions.	**18** Students should summarize their findings and draw conclusions.	**19** Students should reflect upon their data and determine if they want to make changes to eating habits.	**20** Have students turn in their portfolios (see Product Rubric).

Note: This is a project that will not require class time every day. Students will be doing most of the work at home.

How to Track Calories

Tell students that because they will be tracking the amount of calories they eat in a day over the course of a few weeks, it is important to know where to find such information.

Put random amounts of M&Ms in small paper cups and distribute them to the students. Tell students: *You should have a paper cup full of M&Ms in front of you. How do we figure out how many calories are in each cup? We use the Nutrition Facts found on the back of most products. Unfortunately, this does not tell us how many calories a single M&M is, but using math, we can figure it out.*

According to the Nutrition Facts, there are 210 calories in a serving, and a serving is $\frac{1}{4}$ cup. Approximately 52 M&Ms fit into $\frac{1}{4}$ cup. In order to determine how many calories in a single M&M: $210 \div 52 = 4.03$.

Tell students: *Each M&M is approximately 4 calories. To figure out how many calories you are eating, you multiply the number of M&Ms in your cup by 4. If you have 13 M&Ms in your cup, the formula would look like: $13 \times 4 = 52$ calories. You would have to record 52 calories in your log.*

In addition to calories, students will need to record two other aspects of nutrition, such as protein, sodium, sugars, cholesterol, or saturated fats. They can decide which aspects, but they need to focus on the same two for the entire project.

They will need to record their intake for each day in a chart such as this:

Food	Quantity	Calories	Grams of Sugar	Grams of Protein
M&Ms	13	52	6.5	.5
Milk	2 cups	200	24	0
Pizza	3 slices	510	42	6
Orange	1	81	14	2
Big Mac	1	560	8	25
French Fries	1 large	560	0	6
Pepsi	Medium	300	82	0
Total		2,263	176.5	39.5

How to Create Graphs

Picture Graphs

A picture graph uses visuals or symbols to represent numbers. Share with students an example like the picture graph on Handout 10.1, which recorded the amount of grams of sugar per day. Students will need to choose a set of data they wish to display in a picture graph. They can even choose to do all of the items they are tracking if they want to.

Bar Graphs

Bar graphs are a good display when making comparisons between two sets of data. Share with students an example like the bar graph on Handout 10.1, which records calorie consumption for 4 weeks. Point out key elements of the bar graph: the title, key, x-axis, y-axis, and the labels.

Distribute Handout 10.1: Using Graphs, allowing students time to complete the questions. As students develop their own graphs for their portfolios, they will need to create and solve several one- and two-step "how many more" and "how many fewer" questions (like Questions 14 and 15), using information presented in their bar graph.

HANDOUT 10.1

Using Graphs

Directions: Using the graphs provided, answer the questions.

Sugar Consumption	
Day	**Grams of Sugar**
Monday	🛍🛍🛍🛍🛍🛍🛍🛍🛍🛍🛍🛍🛍🛍
Tuesday	🛍🛍🛍🛍🛍🛍🛍
Wednesday	🛍🛍🛍🛍🛍🛍🛍🛍🛍
Thursday	🛍🛍🛍
Friday	🛍🛍🛍🛍🛍
Saturday	🛍🛍
Sunday	🛍🛍🛍
Total	🛍 = 20 grams sugar

1. On which day was the most sugar consumed?

2. On which day was the least sugar consumed?

3. Approximately how much sugar was consumed on Friday?

4. How many more grams of sugar were consumed on Wednesday than there were on Thursday?

5. How many fewer grams of sugar were consumed on Saturday compared to Sunday?

6. Are there any patterns you notice in the data?

Handout 10.1: Using Graphs, *continued*

Calorie Consumption

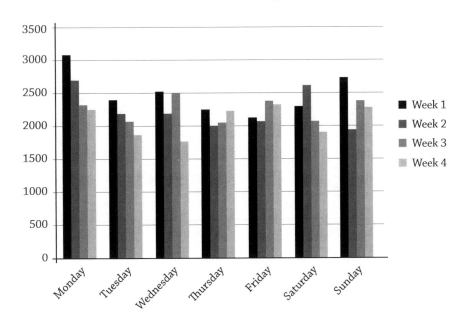

7. On which day and week did the highest consumption of calories take place?

8. On which day and week did the lowest consumption of calories take place?

9. Approximately how many calories were consumed on Saturday, Week 3?

10. On average approximately how many calories were consumed on Fridays?

Handout 10.1: Using Graphs, *continued*

11. Which week had the most calories consumed?

12. Approximately how many calories were consumed in Week 2?

13. Which day of the week seems to have the highest calorie consumption?

14. Looking at Wednesday, how many more calories were consumed during Week 1 as compared to Week 4?

15. Looking at Sundays, how many fewer calories were consumed during Week 2 compared with Week 3?

16. What patterns do you see in the data?

HANDOUT 10.2

Student Reflection

Directions: Once all of the data has been collected, you will need to analyze it and draw conclusions, answering the following questions.

1. What patterns did you notice in your eating habits?

2. Was there anything that surprised you?

3. What did you eat the most of? Was this surprising to you?

4. Do you have a good balance of foods or do you eat the same things over and over?

5. Did your intake of various nutrition stay steady or fluctuate up and down? Why do you suppose this was?

6. How did your average intake compare with recommended intake for someone your age? What did you think of those results?

Handout 10.2: Student Reflection, *continued*

7. Did you notice yourself making any changes in your eating habits during the process of recording your food?

8. Did you family find themselves taking a closer look at their eating habits once you started to keep track of your nutrition intake?

9. Do you think you will make any changes in your eating habits now that the recording of your food is over?

10. How does your calorie intake compare with others who participated?

11. Of the other items you kept track of, were any of them higher or lower than you thought they would be?

12. Do you think you will give more consideration to what you are eating after this project?

13. Did you think it was valuable for you to keep track of your food intake like you did?

Name: _____ Date: _____

PRODUCT RUBRIC

You Are What You Eat

Overall	Portfolio	Data Display	Summary/Reflection
Excellent (A)	◆ Portfolio has 21 complete entries of nutrition facts consumed. ◆ Portfolio is organized and easy to follow. ◆ Portfolio contains a picture graph and bar graph that track the consumption of several nutrition facts over time.	◆ Picture graph looks professional and represents a clear data set with several categories. ◆ Bar graph looks professional and represents a clear data set with several categories.	◆ Student answers all of the reflection questions with detail, specific examples, and insight. ◆ Student has several one- and two-step "how many more" and "how many fewer" problems, using information presented in scaled bar graphs.
Good (B–C)	◆ Portfolio has 21 entries of nutrition facts consumed, but a few are incomplete. ◆ Portfolio is organized but skips parts occasionally and it is not always easy to follow. ◆ Portfolio contains a picture graph and bar graph that track the consumption of several nutrition facts over time, but they are inconsistent or incomplete.	◆ Picture graph represents a data set, but it does not look professional and/or has limited categories. ◆ Bar graph represents a data set, but it does not look professional and/or has limited categories.	◆ Student answers all of the questions in the summary but could use more detail, insight, and/or specific examples. ◆ Student has a few one- and two-step "how many more" and "how many fewer" problems, using information presented in scaled bar graphs.
Needs Work (D–F)	◆ Portfolio does not have 21 entries of nutrition facts consumed. ◆ Portfolio is not organized, making it difficult to determine what the student ate on any given day. ◆ Portfolio either does not contain a picture graph and/or a bar graph, or only tracks one item of nutrition facts over time.	◆ Picture graph is not scaled, making the data collected incorrect. ◆ Bar graph is not scaled, making the data collected incorrect.	◆ Student does not answer all of the questions in the summary and/or has a complete lack of detail, insight, and/or specific examples. ◆ Student has none or only a single one- and two-step "how many more" and "how many fewer" problems.

REFERENCES

Bastiaens, T. J., & Martens, R. L. (2000). Conditions for web-based learning with real events. In B. Abbey (Ed.), *Instructional and cognitive impacts of web-based education* (pp. 1–31). Hershey, PA: Idea Group Publishing.

Brydon, S. R., & Scott, M. D. (2000). *Between one and many: The art and science of public speaking* (3rd ed.). Mountain View, CA: Mayfield.

Dunn, R., Dunn, K., & Price, G. E. (1984). *Learning style inventory.* Lawrence, KS: Price Systems.

Grant, M. M., & Branch, R. M. (2005). Project-based learning in middle school: Tracing abilities through the artifacts of learning. *Journal of Research on Technology in Education, 38,* 65–98.

Horton, R. M., Hedetniemi, T., Wiegert, E., & Wagner, J. R. (2006). Integrating curriculum through themes. *Mathematics Teaching in the Middle School, 11,* 408–414.

Jacobs, L. F., & Hyman, J. S. (2010). *15 Strategies for giving oral presentations.* Retrieved from http://www.usnews.com/education/blogs/professors-guide/2010/02/24/15-strategies-for-giving-oral-presentations

Johnsen-Harris, M. A. (1983). Surviving the budget crunch from an independent school perspective. *Roeper Review, 6,* 79–81.

Johnston, D. E. (2004). Measurement, scale, and theater arts. *Mathematics Teaching in the Middle School, 9,* 412–417.

Jones, G., & Kalinowski, K. (2007). Touring Mars online, real-time, in 3-D, for math and science educators and students. *Journal of Computers in Mathematics and Science Teaching, 26,* 123–136.

Kelly, M. (2014). *Student portfolios: Getting started with student portfolios.* Retrieved from http://712educators.about.com/od/portfolios/a/portfolios.htm

Kingsley, R. F. (1986). "Digging" for understanding and significance: A high school enrichment model. *Roeper Review, 9,* 37–38.

Ljung, E. J., & Blackwell, M. (1996). Project OMEGA: A winning approach for at-risk teens. *Illinois School Research and Development Journal, 33*(1), 15–17.

McMiller, T., Lee, T., Saroop, R., Green, T., & Johnson, C. M. (2006). Middle/high school students in the research laboratory: A summer internship program emphasizing the interdisciplinary nature of biology. *Biochemistry and Molecular Biology Education, 34,* 88–93.

Peterson, M. (1997). Skills to enhance problem-based learning. *Medical Education Online, 2*(3). Retrieved from http://med-ed-online.net/index.php/meo/article/view/4289

Renzulli, J. S., Smith, L. H., & Reis, S. M. (1982). Curriculum compacting: An essential strategy for working with gifted students. *The Elementary School Journal, 82,* 185–194.

Scholastic News Kids Press Corps. (n.d.). *How to conduct a journalistic interview.* Retrieved from http://www.scholastic.com/teachers/article/how-conduct-journalistic-interview

Sedita, J. (2012). *The key comprehension routine: Grades 4–12* (2nd ed.). Rowley, MA: Keys to Literacy.

Stanley, T. (2011). *Project-based learning for gifted students: A handbook for the 21st-century classroom.* Waco, TX: Prufrock Press.

Stanley, T. (2014). *Performance-based assessment for 21st-century skills.* Waco, TX: Prufrock Press.

Stewart, E. D. (1981). Learning styles among gifted/talented students: Instructional technique preferences. *Exceptional Children, 48,* 134–138.

Stoof, A., Martens, R. L., Van Merriënboer, J. J. G., & Bastiaens, T. J. (2002). The boundary approach of competence: A constructivist aid for understanding and using the concept of competence. *Human Resource Development Review, 1*(3), 345–365.

Toolin, R. E. (2004). Striking a balance between innovation and standards: A study of teachers implementing project-based approaches to teaching science. *Journal of Science Education and Technology, 13,* 179–187.

Trilling, B., & Fadel, C. (2009). *21st-century skills: Learning for life in our times.* Hoboken, NJ: Jossey-Bass.

Wagner, T. (2014). *The global achievement gap: Why even our best schools don't teach the new survival skills our children need—and what we can do about it*. New York, NY: Basics Books.

Whitener, E. M. (1989). A meta-analytic review of the effect of learning on the interaction between prior achievement and instructional support. *Review of Educational Research, 59*, 65–86.

ANSWER KEY

Handout 1.2: Fractions

1.

2.

3.

4.

5.

6.

7.

8.

Handout 1.3: Different Denominators

1. 1

2. $1\frac{5}{12}$

3. $1\frac{2}{15}$

4. $1\frac{1}{12}$

5. $\frac{9}{10}$

6. $1\frac{2}{3}$

7. $\frac{5}{6}$

8. $1\frac{7}{20}$

9. $1\frac{1}{5}$

10. $2\frac{1}{10}$

Handout 1.4: Multiplying Fractions by Whole Numbers

1. 1

2. $2\frac{2}{5}$

3. $3\frac{1}{3}$

4. $2\frac{1}{4}$

5. 3

6. $2\frac{1}{3}$

7. $2\frac{2}{5}$

8. 2

9. 2

10. 6

Handout 2.1: Volume

1. 24
2. 8
3. 24
4. 14
5. 30
6. 30

Handout 3.3: How Much Supplies Weigh

1. 17,739 lbs
2. 8,046.27 kg
3. 8,046,270 g
4. 243.83 kg per person
5. 297 lbs of meat
6. 288 lbs of meat

Handout 4.1: Decimals

1. 593.9500
   98.9010
   3013.4000
   402.4021
   73.0000
   275.3010

2. a. 285.976; b. 80.745; c. 521.2; d. 6826.308
3. a. 511.864; b. 8533.67; c. 3711.502; d. 53.568
4. a. 351.016; b. 6938.76; c. 104.300; d. 39494.388
5. a. 6.2; b. 6.52; c. 1.5; d. 594.795

Handout 4.2: Sales Tax and Discounts

1. $476.81
2. $3.40
3. $1.05
4. $16,446.51
5. $18.40
6. $119.74
7. $19.52
8. $764.99
9. $0.38
10. $257,300.08

Handout 6.1: Determining Points on a Coordinate Plane

1. (5, -2)
2. (6, 6)
3. (-1, 4)
4. (-2, -4)
5. (2, 0)
6. (-4, 3)

Handout 6.2: Plotting Continents

1. Africa
2. Asia
3. North America
4. Antarctica
5. North America
6. Europe
7. South America
8. Africa
9. South America
10. Australia

Handout 7.1: Perimeter and Area

1.
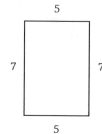

P = 24

2.

P = 16

3.
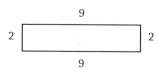

P = 22

4.
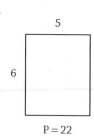

P = 22

5.
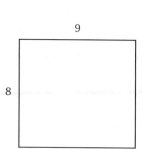

P = 34

6.
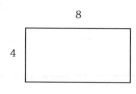

P = 24

7. 110 ft²
8. 18 ft²
9. 36 ft²
10. Answers will vary.
11. Answers will vary.

Handout 9.3: Conversions

1. 63 in
2. 215 in
3. 115 in
4. 301 in
5. 5.8674 m
6. 1.8288 m
7. 0.7366 m
8. 13.2334 m
9. a. 586.74; b. 5867.4; c. .0058674
10. a. 182.88; b. 1828.8; c. .0018288
11. a. 73.66; b. 736.6; c. .0007366
12. a. 1323.34; b. 13233.4; c. .0132334

Handout 10.1: Using Graphs

1. Monday
2. Saturday
3. Approximately 100 g
4. 120 g
5. 20 g
6. Answers will vary.
7. Monday, Week 1
8. Wednesday, Week 4
9. 2,048 calories
10. 2,224 calories
11. Week 1
12. 15,660 calories
13. Monday
14. 735 calories
15. 439 calories
16. Answers will vary.

ABOUT THE AUTHOR

Todd Stanley is the author of seven teacher education books including *Project-Based Learning for Gifted Students: A Handbook for the 21st-Century Classroom* and *Performance-Based Assessment for 21st-Century Skills*. He was a classroom teacher for 19 years, teaching students as young as second graders and as old as high school seniors, and was a National Board Certified teacher. He helped create a gifted academy for grades 5–8, which employs inquiry-based learning, project-based learning, and performance-based assessment. He is currently gifted services coordinator for Pickerington Local School District, OH, where he lives with his wife, Nicki, and two daughters, Anna and Abby.

COMMON CORE STATE STANDARDS ALIGNMENT

Project	Common Core State Standards
Project 1	4.NF.A.1 Explain why a fraction a/b is equivalent to a fraction (n × a)/(n × b) by using visual fraction models, with attention to how the number and size of the parts differ even though the two fractions themselves are the same size. Use this principle to recognize and generate equivalent fractions. 4.NF.A.2 Compare two fractions with different numerators and different denominators, e.g., by creating common denominators or numerators, or by comparing to a benchmark fraction such as 1/2. Recognize that comparisons are valid only when the two fractions refer to the same whole. Record the results of comparisons with symbols >, =, or <, and justify the conclusions, e.g., by using a visual fraction model. 4.NF.B.3 Understand a fraction a/b with a > 1 as a sum of fractions 1/b. 4.NF.B.4 Apply and extend previous understandings of multiplication to multiply a fraction by a whole number.
Project 2	5.MD.C.4 Measure volumes by counting unit cubes, using cubic cm, cubic in, cubic ft, and improvised units. 5.MD.C.5 Relate volume to the operations of multiplication and addition and solve real world and mathematical problems involving volume.

Project	Common Core State Standards
Project 2, *continued*	5.MD.C.5c Recognize volume as additive. Find volumes of solid figures composed of two non-overlapping right rectangular prisms by adding the volumes of the non-overlapping parts, applying this technique to solve real world problems.
Project 3	3.MD.A.1 Tell and write time to the nearest minute and measure time intervals in minutes. Solve word problems involving addition and subtraction of time intervals in minutes, e.g., by representing the problem on a number line diagram. 3.MD.A.2 Measure and estimate liquid volumes and masses of objects using standard units of grams (g), kilograms (kg), and liters (l).1 Add, subtract, multiply, or divide to solve one-step word problems involving masses or volumes that are given in the same units, e.g., by using drawings (such as a beaker with a measurement scale) to represent the problem.
Project 4	5.NBT.B.7 Add, subtract, multiply, and divide decimals to hundredths, using concrete models or drawings and strategies based on place value, properties of operations, and/or the relationship between addition and subtraction; relate the strategy to a written method and explain the reasoning used.
Project 5	4.G.A.1 Draw points, lines, line segments, rays, angles (right, acute, obtuse), and perpendicular and parallel lines. Identify these in two-dimensional figures.
Project 6	5.G.A.1 Use a pair of perpendicular number lines, called axes, to define a coordinate system, with the intersection of the lines (the origin) arranged to coincide with the 0 on each line and a given point in the plane located by using an ordered pair of numbers, called its coordinates. Understand that the first number indicates how far to travel from the origin in the direction of one axis, and the second number indicates how far to travel in the direction of the second axis, with the convention that the names of the two axes and the coordinates correspond (e.g., x-axis and x-coordinate, y-axis and y-coordinate).

Project	Common Core State Standards
Project 6, *continued*	5.G.A.2 Represent real world and mathematical problems by graphing points in the first quadrant of the coordinate plane, and interpret coordinate values of points in the context of the situation.
Project 7	3.MD.D.8 Solve real world and mathematical problems involving perimeters of polygons, including finding the perimeter given the side lengths, finding an unknown side length, and exhibiting rectangles with the same perimeter and different areas or with the same area and different perimeters. 4.MD.A.3 Apply the area and perimeter formulas for rectangles in real world and mathematical problems. For example, find the width of a rectangular room given the area of the flooring and the length, by viewing the area formula as a multiplication equation with an unknown factor.
Project 8	3.NBT.A.3 Multiply one-digit whole numbers by multiples of 10 in the range 10–90 (e.g., 9×80, 5×60) using strategies based on place value and properties of operations. 4.NBT.A.3 Use place value understanding to round multi-digit whole numbers to any place. 5.NBT.A.2 Explain patterns in the number of zeros of the product when multiplying a number by powers of 10, and explain patterns in the placement of the decimal point when a decimal is multiplied or divided by a power of 10. Use whole-number exponents to denote powers of 10.
Project 9	3.MD.B.4 Generate measurement data by measuring lengths using rulers marked with halves and fourths of an inch. Show the data by making a line plot, where the horizontal scale is marked off in appropriate units—whole numbers, halves, or quarters. 4.MD.A.1 Know relative sizes of measurement units within one system of units including km, m, cm; kg, g; lb, oz.; l, ml; hr, min, sec. Within a single system of measurement, express measurements in a larger unit in terms of a smaller unit. Record measurement equivalents in a two-column table.

Project	Common Core State Standards
Project 10	3.MD.B.3 Draw a scaled picture graph and a scaled bar graph to represent a data set with several categories. Solve one- and two-step "how many more" and "how many less" problems using information presented in scaled bar graphs.